New Directions in U.S. National Security Strategy, Defense Plans, and Diplomacy

A REVIEW OF OFFICIAL STRATEGIC DOCUMENTS

Published by Books Express Publishing
Copyright © Books Express, 2011
ISBN 978-1-78039-557-9

Books Express publications are available from all good retail and online booksellers. For
publishing proposals and direct ordering please contact us at: info@books-express.com

New Directions in U.S. National Security Strategy, Defense Plans, and Diplomacy

A REVIEW OF OFFICIAL STRATEGIC DOCUMENTS

By Richard L. Kugler

Published for the Center for Technology
and National Security Policy
Institute for National Strategic Studies
By National Defense University Press
Washington, D.C.
2011

NDU
Press

CONTENTS —————————————————

Where are U.S. national security strategy, defense plans, and diplomacy headed in the coming years? One answer to this important question comes from seven official studies issued in 2010. These studies provide an impressive welter of goals and activities, and they announce major innovations in U.S. policies. But they are hard to absorb in a single setting, and their interrelationships can be hard to determine unless viewed together. To help readers better understand them, this book assembles them into a single exposition, thereby providing "one stop shopping." It describes them individually, shows how they blend together, and evaluates their strengths and limitations.

Five of these studies were written by the U.S. Government, and two were written by teams of independent experts, working with official sponsorship. The studies are:

- *National Security Strategy* (NSS 2010), issued by the White House in May 2010

- *Quadrennial Defense Review Report* (QDR Report), issued by the Department of Defense (DOD) in February 2010

- *The QDR in Perspective: Meeting America's National Security Needs in the 21ˢᵗ Century* (QDRP Report), mandated by Congress and DOD and issued by an independent study group in August 2010

- *Nuclear Posture Review Report* (NPR Report), issued by DOD in April 2010

- *Ballistic Missile Defense Review Report* (BMDR Report), issued by DOD in February 2010

- *NATO 2020: Assured Security; Dynamic Engagement* (ASDE Report), issued by the North Atlantic Treaty Organization (NATO) Group of Experts in May 2010

- *Leading Through Civilian Power: The First Quadrennial Diplomacy and Development Review* (QDDR Report), issued by the Department of State in December 2010.

Separate Reports That Forge a Comprehensive Blueprint. While each of these studies deserves to be treated on its own merits, they are collectively important as they create a comprehensive blueprint for how future U.S. security efforts are to evolve. Together, they argue that if their policies are pursued in tandem, the United States can protect its homeland, advance its interests abroad, be prepared for future missions, help defend its allies, and dampen dangerous international trends while preserving peace and preventing war. NSS 2010 puts forth a new strategy that employs American economic renewal and a "whole of government" approach as engines for driving an assertive, refocused strategy of engagement abroad for handling today's challenges and shaping a stable future international security order. Although NSS 2010 was issued ex post facto a few months after several of the other reports were published, it provides an overarching political framework for appraising how the other six studies of defense strategies and diplomacy fit together. The QDR Report puts forth a new agenda for U.S. conventional defense plans that emphasizes improvements to capabilities for current wars while maintaining flexible and adaptable forces for the future. The QDRP Report—a critique of the QDR Report—calls for an improved force-sizing construct, a larger Navy, more vigorous modernization, and reforms to the weapons-acquisition process. The NPR Report calls for strong policies to prevent nuclear proliferation and nuclear terrorism, reduces the role that nuclear weapons play in U.S. defense strategy, endorses the New Strategic Arms Reduction Treaty (START), and preserves a smaller but modernizing nuclear triad posture. The BMDR Report puts forth a sea-change in U.S. strategy by calling for widespread deployment of SM–3 missile interceptors in order to provide stronger regional missile defenses and security architectures in Europe, the Middle East, and Asia. The ASDE Report calls for NATO to adopt a new strategic concept and to improve its capabilities for expeditionary missions, cyber defense, and other new missions. The QDDR

Report calls for sweeping reforms of the State Department and U.S. Agency for International Development in order to do a better job of carrying out U.S. diplomacy and development policies in troubled regions.

Lingering Issues. All of these studies are well written and cogently argued, but all leave unresolved issues in their wake. In addition to not fully addressing global political constraints ahead, the NSS 2010 does not provide enough analysis of regional priorities, adequately treat the risk of big-power competition, or address strategy options if Iran acquires nuclear weapons. The QDR Report fails to give full attention to long-term imperatives including force requirements, joint operations, and modernization. The QDRP Report fails to address how a larger Navy and a more robust modernization plan are to be funded. The NPR Report does not provide enough analysis showing whether its counterproliferation policies will succeed, and does not specify how additional nuclear force reductions beyond New START can unfold. The BMDR Report endorsement of regional SM–3 deployments is predicated on the assumption that regional allies and partners will agree with U.S. deployment plans. The ASDE Report agenda for improving NATO capabilities does not take into account the negative effects of austerity budgets and defense cutbacks across Europe. The QDDR Report fails to adequately address substantive priorities for diplomacy and development policies in troubled regions and to analyze how classical diplomacy—for example, big-power relations—will need to change.

Future Analytical Challenges. While the seven studies equip U.S. national security strategy and defense plans with new goals, policies, and priorities, they do not preclude the need for further thinking, analyzing, and refining. For example, they will require additional attention to the challenges of creating new regional security architectures in Europe, Asia, and the Middle East. Thus, they open the door to a new era of studies and analyses whose dimensions are only beginning to be understood.

Where are U.S. national security strategy, defense plans, and diplomacy headed in the coming years? An answer to this important question comes from seven official studies that have been issued during 2010. This volume assembles these studies into a common framework, examines their individual contents, shows how they work together to forge a comprehensive official blueprint for the future, and evaluates them individually and collectively. Five of these studies were written by the U.S. Government; two were written by teams of independent experts but had official sponsorship. The studies are:

- *National Security Strategy,* issued by the White House in May 2010
- *Quadrennial Defense Review Report,* issued by the Department of Defense (DOD) in February 2010
- *The QDR in Perspective: Meeting America's National Security Needs in the 21st Century,* mandated by Congress and DOD and issued by an independent study group in August 2010
- *Nuclear Posture Review Report,* issued by DOD in April 2010
- *Ballistic Missile Defense Review Report,* issued by DOD in February 2010
- *NATO 2020: Assured Security; Dynamic Engagement,* issued by the North Atlantic Treaty Organization Group of Experts in May 2010
- *Leading Through Civilian Power: The First Quadrennial Diplomacy and Development Review,* issued by the Department of State in December 2010.

The first study describes the basics of U.S. national security strategy for the coming years, including core goals, concepts, and activities for guiding foreign policy and diplomacy worldwide. The next four studies bore down into the associated details of U.S. defense planning, including conventional and nuclear forces and missile defenses. The sixth study examines the issues surrounding the Alliance's strategic concept and defense improvement plans. The final study analyzes future U.S. diplomacy and development policies, and focuses on reforms to the Department of State and U.S. Agency for International Development internal structures and operations.

While each of these studies has a purpose of its own in ways that demand careful appraisal, they need to be viewed collectively because they are interdependent, and together they aspire to cover much of the waterfront for U.S. security strategy and future directions for defense plans and diplomacy. A collective appraisal can illuminate their interrelationships, show how they form a cohesive whole, and reveal their strengths, shortcomings, and lingering issues. Whereas roughly 75 percent of the following pages are devoted to describing and explaining the seven studies, 25 percent are devoted to critiquing them.

The purpose of this volume is not only to help educate readers, but also to evaluate emerging U.S. strategies, policies, and plans. This work addresses each of these seven studies individually in sequential order. In each case, it endeavors to summarize the main features of the study and to evaluate its contents. At the end, this book examines how these studies interlock to form an overall blueprint, identifies lingering issues that call for further analysis, and offers constructive ideas for further research and analyses.

A main theme emerges from the following pages, one that derives from the highly interactive nature of each of the seven studies. Taken together, these studies provide an impressive edifice of goals, policies, plans, and activities in ways that often surpass earlier official efforts. They aptly illustrate the complex challenges facing the United States, the need to handle them effectively, and the necessity of employing a wide range of instruments, military and civilian. They put forth many fresh ideas and innovative departures—for example, building effective regional missile defenses—even as they foster continuity in areas deemed appropriate. They argue that if their strategies and plans are pursued with energy and adequate resources, the United States can aspire to protect its vital interests and those of its allies in the coming years while also contributing to a stable international order.

Nonetheless, these studies are not perfect, they do not resolve all controversies, and, at times, they seem to create gaps or at least leave unresolved issues in their wake. The task facing the U.S. Government will be one of building upon these studies in order to further strengthen them.

CHAPTER ONE

National Security Strategy

A 52-page document, the National Security Strategy Report of 2010 (NSS 2010) puts forth a new U.S. strategy for national economic renewal, global leadership, and comprehensive engagement aimed at strengthening the capacity for collective action to create a just and sustainable international order that can resolve 21st-century challenges. The document is written in a manner aimed at articulating the rationale, goals, and constituent policies of each component of this ambitious, far reaching strategy, which is global in conception and focused both on the near and long terms. Its strategic approach endeavors to blend the art of the possible with that of fostering the desirable. While acknowledging that the United States must work within the confines of the often stressful world, with its numerous dangers and threats, the NSS 2010 aspires to employ U.S. energy and purpose, in concert with allies and other cooperative partners, in an effort to shape the future in ways that produce a more secure, stable, and prosperous world. Accordingly, the NSS 2010 calls for the United States to remain in a leadership role in global affairs, rather than retreat into disengagement and isolation. Furthermore, it calls upon the United States to harness a wide array of civilian and military instruments, to continue meeting its security commitments to allies, to work closely with many other nations and international institutions, and to deal firmly with adversary nations and other actors that threaten U.S. security interests and global peace. By any measure, this is a strategy anchored in both hopeful goals and commitment to an activist foreign policy and diplomacy, but often in ways that differ from those of the past.

More than earlier strategies, the NSS 2010 places considerable emphasis on renewing America's economic prosperity to create a strong foundation for an assertive national security strategy. Accordingly, it calls for national policies aimed at reducing the deficit, ending recession, and restoring economic growth. It also calls for investments in education, clean energy, infrastructure, technological innovation, and goods and services for export. For similar reasons, it mandates close cooperation with the Group of 20 (G–20) in order to create sustained global economic growth in ways that benefit the U.S. economy. A stronger economy, the NSS 2010 contends, can liberate the resources needed to fund a whole-of-government approach to national security strategy. This approach envisions sustained efforts to strengthen policy implementation by integrating a wide spectrum of means, including diplomatic, informational, military, economic, intelligence, development, homeland security, and strategic communications instruments. Whereas earlier NSS studies often treated defense preparedness as the main instrument of power, the NSS 2010 views military forces as one instrument among many, all of which require appropriate funding as well as strong coordination by the U.S. Government. But it also makes clear that the United States must maintain its military superiority in the form of tailored deterrence strategies and fully sufficient capabilities across all domains— land, sea, air, and cyber—to reassure allies, contend with threats, and otherwise perform core defense missions.

The NSS 2010 defines *engagement* as the active participation by the United States in relationships beyond its borders, and it proposes to carry out engagement more vigorously and in different ways than found in the strategy of the George W. Bush administration (2001–2009). It asserts that comprehensive engagement must begin with close friends and allies, but must reach beyond them to other countries, including great powers and adversaries. While the NSS 2010 makes clear that the United States will retain the right to use military force when necessary, it disavows unilateralism and regular use of force as well as practices, such as torture, that can be viewed as violations of international law. It proclaims that promoting universal values—including democratic practices, respect for human rights, and setting a sound moral example—is highly important to enhancing U.S. influence abroad.

Compared to the Bush administration, it places less emphasis on rapid global democratization as a central engine of progress and is more prone to advance this goal through quiet diplomacy rather than high-profile activity. Its approach to global diplomacy emphasizes that multilateralism and collective action will be a dominant practice in handling both security affairs and the world economy. It calls upon the United States to preserve and reform existing alliances, broaden partnerships, pursue cooperation with such big powers as Russia, China, and India, and work closely with the United Nations and other international organizations. In its view, flourishing multilateral partnerships should be a principal mechanism— more so than in the recent past—for strengthening U.S. influence, mobilizing many nations to address problems from the perspective of common shared interests, and isolating countries and actors that threaten peace.

In deciding how the United States should act abroad, the NSS 2010 views the world as undergoing a major transition propelled by fast-paced changes, heading away from the international order inherited from the Cold War, and moving rapidly toward an unclear destination, which must be proactively shaped by the Nation and its allies. It portrays globalization as a main dynamic drawing previously distant regions and countries closer together in a growing web of economic, political, and information ties. The result, it asserts, is a combination of promising and perilous trends that, while yielding progress in many ways, is encouraging and empowering such dangerous trends as the persistent rise of terrorist groups and the grave threat of nuclear proliferation. In this setting, the NSS 2010 calls for U.S. national security strategy to pursue four enduring national interests:

- security: the security of the United States, its citizens, allies, and partners
- prosperity: a strong, innovative, and growing U.S. economy in an open international economic system that promotes opportunity and prosperity
- values: respect for universal values at home and abroad

- international order: an order advanced by U.S. leadership that promotes peace, security, and opportunity through stronger cooperation to meet global challenges.

Handling Top Security Priorities. The NSS 2010 identifies the following top security priorities for U.S. strategy:

- strengthen security and resilience at home
- disrupt, dismantle, and defeat al Qaeda and its violent extremist affiliates in Afghanistan, Pakistan, and around the world
- reverse the spread of nuclear and biological weapons and secure nuclear materials
- advance peace, security, and opportunity in the Greater Middle East
- invest in the capacity of strong and capable partners
- secure cyberspace.

To strengthen security and resilience at home, the NSS 2010 calls for such steps as preventing and interdicting threats, denying hostile actors the ability to operate within U.S. borders, doing a better job of reducing vulnerabilities to the national infrastructure as well borders, ports, and airfields, and enhancing overall air, maritime, transportation, and space security. It also calls for improved measures to manage emergencies, empower communities to counter radicalization, strengthen Federal-state-local cooperation, and work closely with allies and partners on common homeland security agendas.

To wage a global campaign against al Qaeda and its terrorist affiliates, the NSS 2010 earmarks the importance of homeland security measures, but it attaches special emphasis to defeating al Qaeda in Afghanistan and Pakistan. In Afghanistan, it calls for an assertive strategy aimed at denying al Qaeda a safe haven, disallowing the Taliban the ability to overthrow the government, and strengthening the capacity of the Afghanistan government and security forces, so they can take lead responsibility for their future. Within Pakistan, it calls for continuing U.S. efforts to work with the government to address the local, regional, and global threat from violent extremists. In order to attain these objectives in both countries, the NSS 2010 puts forth a three-pronged strategy aimed at:

- employing the U.S. military and International Security Assistance Force to target the insurgency, secure key population centers, and train Afghan security forces
- working with partners and the United Nations to improve Afghan governance and economic conditions
- fostering a relationship with Pakistan founded on mutual interests and mutual respect in ways aimed at both countering terrorists and promoting Pakistan's democratic and economic development.

While the NSS 2010 focuses mainly on Afghanistan and Pakistan, it also calls for growing pressure to deny al Qaeda safe-havens in such places as Yemen, Somalia, the Maghreb, and the Sahel.

The NSS 2010 attaches high priority to reversing the spread of nuclear weapons and materials as well as biological weapons. It calls for intensified efforts to pursue the goal of a world without nuclear weapons through such steps as strengthening the Non-Proliferation Treaty (NPT), ratifying the New Strategic Arms Reduction Treaty (START) with Russia, ratifying the Comprehensive Test Ban Treaty, and pursuing a new treaty that verifiably ends the production of nuclear materials intended for use in weapons. It views the basic bargain of the NPT as still valid: countries with nuclear weapons will move toward disarmament, countries without nuclear weapons will forsake them, and all countries can access peaceful nuclear energy. The NSS 2010 also calls for presenting a clear choice to Iran and North Korea: either accept denuclearization or face isolation from the international community. In addition, it puts forth policies aimed at securing nuclear weapons and materials, supporting peaceful nuclear energy, and countering biological threats. In particular, it cites the Proliferation Security Initiative and the Global Initiative to Combat Nuclear Terrorism as programs that should be expanded into durable international efforts.

Proclaiming that the United States has important interests in the Greater Middle East that include stable security affairs and political-economic progress, the NSS 2010 calls for an American engagement that is both comprehensive and strategic and that extends beyond near-term threats to include long-term development. In Iraq, it calls for a responsible transition to full Iraqi responsibility as U.S. forces withdraw by the end of 2011. As the war in Iraq ends, it promises strong U.S. civilian support for the country, led by the State Department, coupled with a regional diplomacy aimed at ensuring that Iraq emerges as stable, secure, and prosperous with a competent, democratic government.

The NSS 2010 also calls for vigorous efforts to promote Arab-Israeli peace rooted in a two-state solution for Palestine and Israel, as well as better Israeli relations with Syria and Lebanon. To promote a responsible Iran, the NSS 2010 calls for a U.S. policy of engagement in hope that Iran will switch course away from threatening behavior and toward constructive participation in regional and global affairs. But it also warns that if Iran fails to respond positively, it will face even greater isolation.

Through the lens of the NSS 2010, the practice of investing in the capacity of strong and durable partners refers to efforts aimed at helping failed and failing states to surmount their internal problems, achieve political-economic progress, and resist radicalization and extremism. This agenda has three components: fostering security and reconstruction in the aftermath of conflict, pursuing sustainable and responsible security systems in at-risk states, and preventing the emergence of conflict by promoting long-term development. The desired outcome is not only restored stable states but also close friends and partners of the United States. The NSS 2010 cites Iraq and Afghanistan as the top near-term priorities for this type of involvement, but its open-ended discussion suggests potential involvements elsewhere when failing states have strategic importance. The implication is that even if the United States ultimately withdraws from Iraq and Afghanistan, it will be in the business of stabilization, reconstruction, and comprehensive approaches for a long time.

The final security priority cited by the NSS 2010 is securing cyberspace. Stating that the national digital infrastructure is a vital strategic asset, the NSS 2010 identifies cyber threats from a wide spectrum of sources: individual hackers, criminal groups, terrorist networks, and advanced hostile nations. It demonstrates particular concern about major cyber attacks that could cause crippling damage to the U.S. Government, economy, and military forces. To protect U.S information networks, the NSS 2010 calls for close cooperation among the government, industry, and private citizens. It also calls for similar cooperation with partner nations to prevent cyber attacks, deal effectively with them when they occur, and recover promptly.

Promoting Prosperity and Values. The NSS 2010 mainly views prosperity in terms of restoring sustained growth to the U.S. economy, but it calls for policies aimed at fostering growth by the international economy as well. It views pursuit of a healthy global economy and stable security affairs as interconnected and mutually reinforcing. It argues that the free flow of commerce advances peace among nations by making them more integrated, prosperous, and stable. Conversely, it argues that disastrous shocks to the world economy, slowdowns, and recessions can damage prosperity in many places and help make security affairs more intractable. The challenge facing the United States, it reasons, is not only to make its own economy more competitive in the world economy, but also to help steer the world economy toward open trade, expanding markets, financial stability, and sustained growth enjoyed by as many countries as possible.

To achieve balanced and sustainable growth for the U.S. and global economy, the NSS 2010 calls for U.S.-led efforts to prevent economic imbalances and financial excesses. It also calls for efforts to increase U.S. exports while encouraging other countries to import more U.S. products and services, shift to greater domestic demand abroad, enhance the performance of such international institutions as the G–20, World Bank, and International Monetary Fund (IMF), and dampen international economic crime. In addition, the NSS 2010 acknowledges awareness that the world economy is becoming two-tiered—with Europe, Asia, China, and India experiencing steady growth, but other regions lagging behind. Accordingly, it calls for assistance policies that can help make poor countries more prosperous. It particularly cites sub-Saharan Africa as needing economic and development assistance in several areas, including good governance, improvements to agriculture, and health care.

In its treatment of values, the NSS 2010 asserts that because the United States believes some values are universal, including democracy and human rights, it should work to promote them worldwide. Promoting them in effective ways makes sense, it states, not only for idealistic reasons, but also because the spread of these values encourages peace, international cooperation, and a friendly stance toward the United States. The problem today, it further states, is that the spread of democracy and humans rights has stalled in worrisome ways. It points out that whereas some autocratic governments have suppressed democracy and human rights in the name of economic modernity and national unity, some authoritarian governments, while brandishing ostensibly democratic credentials, have taken such steps as impeding the electoral process and undermining civil society. Such trends, it argues, are not worldwide, but are prevalent in enough regions to spell trouble for the continued spread of democracy and human rights.

Faced with this challenge, the NSS 2010 states, the United States can best respond by setting a powerful example. Accordingly, it calls for policies that prohibit torture, counter terrorism legally, balance the imperatives of secrecy and transparency, protect civil liberties, uphold the rule of law, and draw strength from diversity. In acting abroad, it states, the United States should strive to ensure that new and fragile democracies deliver tangible improvements for their citizens. In dealing with nondemocratic regimes, the NSS 2010 endorses principled engagement in the form of a dual-track approach. This requires the United States to improve government-to-government relations and use the resulting dialogue to advance human rights, while engaging civil society and peaceful political opposition. In addition, it calls for U.S. policies that recognize the legitimacy of all peaceful democratic movements, support women's rights, strengthen international norms against corruption, build broader coalitions to advance universal values, and promote the right to access information. Finally, it calls for efforts to promote human dignity by meeting such basic needs as health care and access to food.

Promoting International Order. The NSS 2010 calls for creation of an international order that is not only just and sustainable, but also capable of handing the new challenges of the 21st century. Anchored in the premise that the international architecture inherited from the Cold War is breaking down, it asserts that a new international order must bind nations together in a web of shared interests, accepted rules of the road, a commitment to collective action, multinational institutions, and common strategies—all of which provide a growing capacity to handle such new-era challenges as terrorism, nuclear proliferation, regional conflicts, economic troubles, climate change, pandemic disease, and international crime.

As used by NSS 2010, the term *international order* does not refer to a single hierarchical structure in the manner of the United Nations, but instead implies a functioning, flexible cluster of likeminded nations that choose to act together in pursuit of their common interests. A key feature is that this international order is to be created through cooperation by its member nations, is to be as large and powerful as possible, and is to provide a usable framework for collective action by coalitions focused on handing specific challenges. While acknowledging that creating such an international order will be difficult, the NSS 2010 states that the effort is imperative, and that if the United States leads wisely and works closely with likeminded nations, progress is achievable. It further states that unless such an international order is created, the forces of instability and disorder will undermine global security. Accordingly, the NSS 2010 puts forth a four-part plan for this endeavor:

- ensure strong alliances
- build cooperation with other 21st-century centers of influence
- strengthen institutions and mechanisms for cooperation
- sustain broad cooperation on key global challenges.

As articulated by the NSS 2010, America's security alliances, especially those in Europe and Asia, will provide a strong foundation for the new international order. The NSS 2010 argues that these alliances—and their resulting patterns of close cooperation among the United States and its many allies—provide potent force multipliers that permit participants to pursue more demanding security goals than otherwise would be possible by those members acting alone. The NSS 2010 also makes clear that the Nation will continue participating in these alliances in traditional ways, including multilateral defense planning and stronger regional deterrence postures, aimed at protecting their security against old and new threats. But it also states that the United States will lead efforts to revitalize and reform these alliances so that they can handle new challenges.

In Europe, the NSS 2010 calls for U.S. policies aimed at preserving the North Atlantic Treaty Organization (NATO) as a vibrant, revitalized, and effective alliance that can handle the full range of 21st-century security challenges, while partnering with the European Union to bring security and democracy to Eastern Europe and the Balkans, and to resolve conflicts in the Caucasus and Cyprus. It states that NATO's new strategic concept will provide an opportunity to pursue alliance reforms, but it does not specify what such reforms should include. In Asia, the NSS 2010 calls for policies aimed at deepening and updating U.S. alliances with Japan, South Korea, Australia, the Philippines, and Thailand to reflect new-era Asian dynamics while preserving security and promoting prosperity for those countries. It particularly emphasizes U.S. efforts to modernize alliances with Japan and Korea in order to face evolving security challenges, foster equal relationships, and preserve a solid foundation for the continuing presence of U.S. military forces there. The NSS 2010 also cites America's close relations with Canada and Mexico as central to North American security and economic progress.

The NSS 2010's call for building cooperation with other 21st-century centers of influence reflects awareness that several countries and regions are acquiring greater power and asserting themselves more aggressively on the world stage. It singles out China, India, and Russia as key actors with whom the United States needs cooperative bilateral relationships for addressing common problems. It cites the rise of the G–20 as an example of the growing shift toward greater cooperation between traditional powers and emerging centers of influence. It identifies Asia as an entire region that is acquiring greater economic and political weight in world affairs. It calls for deep, enduring, and growing U.S. ties with countries of the region anchored in mutual interests, close security collaboration with friends and allies, flourishing economic and trade relations aimed at enhancing American exports, and cooperation with such multilateral Asian institutions as the Association of Southeast Asian Nations (ASEAN), Asia Pacific Economic Forum, Trans-Pacific Partnership, and the East Asia Summit.

The NSS 2010's approach to China reflects the region-wide U.S. strategy in Asia. It seeks a positive, constructive, and comprehensive relationship with China. While stating that the United States will monitor China's military modernization program to ensure that American allies are not endangered, the NSS 2010 welcomes a China that plays a responsible leadership role in handling security challenges, encourages China to make choices that contribute to peace, security, and prosperity as China's influence grows, and encourages a continued reduction in tensions between China and Taiwan. The NSS 2010 calls for a growing strategic partnership with India based on common interests, shared values, and commitments to help solve key security challenges. The NSS 2010 also asserts that the United States has an abiding interest in a strong, peaceful, and prosperous Russia that respects international norms. While stating that the United States will support the sovereignty and territorial integrity of Russia's neighbors, it calls for a growing partnership with Russia in such critical areas as nuclear arms reductions and confronting violent extremism, especially in Afghanistan. In addition, the NSS 2010 calls attention to the importance of constructive, cooperation-building U.S. policies toward Indonesia, Brazil, friendly Arab countries in the Middle East and Persian Gulf, and South Africa. Across Africa, it urges a strong U.S. engagement focused on assistance policies that help foster good governance, economic development, and conflict resolution.

As part of U.S. strategy for promoting a new international order, the NSS 2010 calls for efforts to strengthen institutions and mechanisms for cooperation. It encourages a more robust and effective United Nations, including Security Council reforms, a more efficient civil service, and strengthened operational capacity for peacekeeping, humanitarian relief, development assistance, and promotion of human rights. It calls for U.S.-led efforts to promote common actions through a wide range of frameworks and coalitions, accompanied by policies to spur and harness a new diversity of instruments and institutions. The emerging division of labor would be based on effectiveness, competency, and long-term reliability. It envisions progress on a host of fronts, including international financial institutions, multilateral development banks, and the IMF as well as leveraged policies for fostering economic progress in poor regions. It also calls for policies aimed at investing in improved regional capabilities, including such bodies as the Organization for Security and Co-operation in Europe, Organization of the Islamic Conference, African Union, Organization of American States, ASEAN, and the Gulf Cooperation Council. In guiding these regional bodies, the NSS 2010 calls for a strategic approach that takes into account a sensible division of roles and responsibilities and that encourages reforms and innovations in order to address emerging security and economic priorities in multiple areas.

Finally, the approach put forth by the NSS 2010 urges sustained, broad, global cooperation on a host of 21st-century challenges that have been resistant to progress in the past. It argues that global cooperation on them is necessary because no single nation, or even group of nations, can handle them alone. It especially focuses on addressing climate change, peacekeeping to control armed conflicts, prevention of genocide and mass atrocities, international justice, pandemics and infectious diseases, world heath, transnational criminal threats, safeguarding the global commons and cyberspace, and access to the Arctic. International cooperation in these areas, the NSS 2010 argues, can help promote progress on difficult challenges that transcend individual regions in ways that often make them truly global.

Strengths, Shortcomings, and Lingering Issues. By any measure, the NSS 2010 is a thorough, articulate, and reasoned document that clearly spells out main directions for future U.S. national security strategy as seen by the Obama administration. Written in a manner evidently designed to capture widespread bipartisan consensus in the American political system, it draws major criticism mostly from opposite ends of the spectrum—that is, some critics see it as too liberal and others as too conservative. If a well-conceived national security strategy is defined as a strategic construct for pursuing multiple goals in complementary ways, the NSS 2010 meets this standard. Judged in such technical terms, it is as good, or better, than similar national security strategy studies written by previous administrations. By being so comprehensive, it performs its intended role of helping to guide the multiple U.S. departments and agencies that play central roles in carrying out national security strategy. It leaves few subjects untouched, even if it sometimes pursues breadth at the expense of depth.

A key strength is that the NSS 2010 defines national security in broad terms that include not only traditional military and security issues, but also the full set of wider issues that animate U.S. foreign policy and diplomacy, including economic policies, political relations with many countries, institutional relationships, and developmental policies in key regions. Focusing on national economic renewal, its whole-of-government approach makes sense in an emerging era in which the success of U.S. national security strategy will be heavily influenced by the availability of resources and the ability of the U.S. Government to orchestrate multiple policy instruments. Emphasis on a strategy of U.S. engagement abroad, coupled with its call for sustained multilateral cooperation, clearly responds favorably to the many allies, partners, and friends abroad looking for this blend of leadership and collaboration from the United States. Its emphasis on working with the G–20 to handle the world economy reflects accelerating globalization dynamics as well as the need for common policies by many nations. Its call for promoting democratic values mainly by the strength of American example and through quiet diplomacy may seem insufficiently assertive to some critics, but it does not coddle dictators. It does reflect an official judgment that this is the best practical way to make progress today.

Virtually all of the dozens of security policy initiatives put forth by NSS 2010 have generated controversy. The best way to evaluate this document is not to ask whether it is correct in its handling of myriad details, but instead to ask whether it correctly judges strategic fundamentals. In this arena, it is fair to observe that in trying to strike a balance between idealism and realism, the NSS 2010's emphasis on shaping the future world, rather than being victimized by unwelcome trends, reflects sound reasoning that has been shared by many past administrations. The notion, thus, is not new; the question is whether, and to what degree, it can be accomplished. Such an analysis needs to be conducted in light of the many frustrations encountered by past administrations when they set out to shape the future of a rapidly evolving world that responds to many complexities, not just American leadership. Whereas optimists might judge that important successes are achievable, pessimists, especially those animated by concern that U.S. power is declining, might judge that the opposite will be true. While the debate between them will be settled only when the future unfolds, what can be said now is that the NSS 2010 strikes a hopeful tone partly because it is preoccupied with spelling out a large set of goals and their supporting policies—in isolation from constraints on pursuing them. Along the way, it does not offer much analysis of whether these goals are feasibly achievable and whether their policies will be strong and agile enough to get the job fully done. To the extent that the NSS 2010 errs in strategic terms, it may be on the side of implying that more can be accomplished than actually will be the case.

In any event, the NSS 2010 puts forth an undeniably ambitious global agenda for the United States to pursue as a leader of many alliances, coalitions, and endeavors. These range from handling the high politics of the global security system and world economy to carrying out gritty wars and reconstruction efforts across the Greater Middle East and adjoining regions. Nowhere does it discuss in any detail limits to America's strategic interests, geographic and functional areas that fall outside these limits, responsibilities that should be carried out by countries other than the United States, and the need to set priorities so that vital goals are attained even at the expense of not achieving less important ones. Critics might judge that, although the NSS 2010 cautions against overextending U.S. foreign involvements, it establishes a sweeping strategy framework that risks falling into this trap. While only the future will tell, an appropriate conclusion is that between the poles of full disengagement and assertive engagement almost everywhere, there is a middle ground that calls for strong but selective engagement on a manageable list of strategic issues where success is both mandatory and achievable. Whether emerging U.S. strategy will find this middle ground is to be seen, but the NSS 2010 does not cause the most vital goals to be highlighted.

The NSS 2010 tries to establish a sense of focus at least for the near term by identifying its six top security priorities. However, questions can be raised about this list and the analyses supporting it. No one would quarrel with the goals of defending the U.S. homeland, defeating al Qaeda and its affiliates, stopping nuclear proliferation, and protecting cyberspace—or with needing to stabilize failed states that have strategic importance. The goals of winding down the war in Iraq while succeeding in Afghanistan are broadly shared across the United States. But the goal of advancing Middle East security and stability is bereft of actionable steps of what should be done if, as seems increasingly possible, Iran acquires nuclear weapons and delivery systems. Assuming that war against Iran is rejected as a viable choice, presumably a U.S.-led containment and deterrence regime would need to be created that compels Iran to keep its nuclear weapons holstered and devoid of major influence across the region. Can such a regime be created, how would it be established, how would it operate, and would it be successful? The NSS 2010 is silent on this vital topic in ways that could neuter its Middle East relevance if Iran indeed becomes a nuclear power. Nor did the NSS 2010 anticipate the wave of revolutions that subsequently broke out in Tunisia, Egypt, Libya, and elsewhere in the Middle East—all of which will need to be factored into new U.S. regional policies as the future unfolds.

Likewise, the priorities offered do not even mention the still paramount goals of keeping Europe and Asia stable and peaceful. If these two huge, powerful regions somehow plunge into instability, they will take the rest of the world with them. By not mentioning them, does the NSS 2010 imply that handling these two regions is no longer serious and demanding enough to be listed as a top security priority? If so, it will be the first major U.S. strategy study to reach such a conclusion in many decades. Part of the problem stems from the NSS 2010's tendency to be so preoccupied with analyzing global trends and policies that, the Middle East aside, it pays insufficient attention to the various regions. Europe and Asia are especially noticeable casualties because they have always figured so prominently in U.S. national security strategy, and still do so in many important ways. The NSS 2010 does briefly examine Europe and Asia as part of its general discussion of creating a new international order. Here, it raises the idea of creating stronger regional deterrence postures in those regions and elsewhere, but it offers no further insights on how this important, consequence-laden idea can be carried out in political-military terms. Its brief treatment invites more questions than answers. Nor does it answer an even more basic question: How are the European and Asian security systems to be structured and operated in the coming years—similar to now, or differently? Failure to answer this question in adequate depth creates a noticeable gap in the NSS 2010.

Moreover, questions can be raised about the NSS 2010's discussion of whether and how a future international security order is to take shape. Clearly, the idea of creating a stronger consensus for managing global challenges makes sense. But as the NSS 2010 acknowledges, a truly expansive international order cannot be imposed from the top. Instead, it must emerge from the bottom up in ways anchored in the mutual interests of participating nations. At issue is whether, in a world of growing pluralism, such a harmonization of interests, especially among the big powers, is possible. Geopolitical theorists aware of history likely would raise doubts by arguing that in an era of intensifying multipolarity, growing big-power competition is more likely than not, and that before something as visionary as a cooperative international order can be created, a stable structure of security affairs—and even a stable balance of power—must first be established.

In its preoccupation with handling such present-day dangers as global terrorism and WMD proliferation, the NSS 2010 tends to presume that today's lack of deep rivalry and competition among the major powers can be taken for granted as an enduring characteristic. But is this a wise presumption? Today's relative tranquility is a historical anomaly that may not be permanent. In the past, settings of amorphous pluralism among big powers have tended to give way to growing political conflict among them, followed by a drift toward tense multipolarity and culminated by a descent into confrontational bipolarity. Is this historical pattern destined to repeat itself? Will such major powers as the United States, Europe, Russia, China, Japan, and India remain at peace, or will they succumb to the experiences of the past by becoming at loggerheads with each other?

Answering this question in forward-looking ways does not require accepting rigid theories of historical determinism. But it does require awareness of underlying geopolitical dynamics at work among the big powers now and in the future. It also requires acceptance of the proposition that preserving stability among the major powers may not be automatic. Instead, it could require hard work by the United States—and if major power rivalry starts taking hold, the United States will have to work even harder to contain it. Pursuing such a difficult agenda would require a U.S. global strategy anchored more heavily in concepts of geopolitical management than now. The NSS 2010 does not provide such concepts. Rather, it remains largely silent on a strategic task that, to one degree or another, could become an increasingly important U.S. preoccupation.

Geopolitical management of the future roles of Russia and China especially enters the strategic equation here because of their power, geographical locations astride Europe and Asia, and capacities for causing both good and ill. Today's reality is that China is rapidly emerging as a regional and global power, and Russia is trying to reassert itself in similar ways. Their future strategic agendas are unclear. However, if China emerges as a menace to the

United States and its allies in Asia, and if Russian reemerges as a menace to Europe and a rival of the United States in the Middle East, both will bring growing troubles to U.S. national security strategy. If these two major powers start acting in ways that require counterbalancing and restraining, it will be the United States that will need to perform this task. Perhaps the NSS 2010 correctly judges that close cooperation with those two countries can predominate and that, apart from taking precautionary steps at the margins as a hedge against relations with them souring, future U.S. strategy need not think in classical geopolitical terms in dealing with them. But if NSS 2010 errs on this score, it risks being wrong on something so basic that the core concept of creating a new international order is rendered far more difficult, and maybe invalid. Indeed, the underlying global security system could become a source of future challenges, not an engine for solving them. In such a more dangerous, less tractable world, U.S. national security strategy would need to be perhaps even fundamentally different from the vision put forth by NSS 2010.

Finally, the NSS 2010 has a gap that flows from one of its main strengths. In its discussion of a whole-of-government approach, it appropriately discusses the key roles that many different policy instruments must play in carrying out not only national security strategy, but also traditional foreign policy and diplomacy. Along the way, it addresses military and defense issues in ways that mainly articulate only basic principles, without discussing in any serious way the details of force posture, improvement plans, overseas presence, employment strategies, and allied military contributions. Nor does it discuss the military forces of adversary nations—indeed, its political treatment of adversaries is mostly confined to North Korea and Iran—or contingencies in which U.S. forces might be involved. Perhaps this absence of deeper treatment is not a weakness given the larger purposes and messages of the document, but previous national security strategy studies typically paid more attention to military affairs. This illuminates the importance of examining those five official studies on military and defense affairs also published in 2010.

Quadrennial Defense Review Report

Written as a complement to the National Security Strategy of 2010 (NSS 2010), the Quadrennial Defense Review (QDR) Report of 2010 is a 105-page document that addresses U.S. defense strategy, force planning, and resource priorities for the coming years including Future Years Defense Plan 2011–2015 and beyond. Claiming to be strategy-driven and analytical, it advances two main objectives: rebalancing the U.S. Armed Forces to prevail in today's wars while preparing to deal with future threats; and reforming Department of Defense (DOD) institutions and processes to better support urgent needs of the warfighter, buy new weapons affordably, and make efficient use of resources. It is mainly preoccupied with conventional forces and preparations; it delegates nuclear and missile defense forces to two subsequent DOD studies (addressed below).

In his memorandum introducing the QDR Report, Secretary of Defense Robert Gates proclaims that because it is a truly wartime document, for the first time, it places current conflicts, especially Afghanistan and Iraq, at the top of DOD priorities. But he also states that because of the simultaneous need to prepare for a wide range of security challenges on the horizon, the United States requires a broad portfolio of military capabilities with maximum versatility across the entire spectrum of potential conflict. To meet those threats to the U.S. military's capacity to project power, deter aggression, and aid allies and partners, Secretary Gates calls for more focus and investments in a new air-sea battle concept, and long-range strike, space, and cyberspace assets, along with other conventional and strategic modernization programs. He also calls for fresh efforts to work closely with allies and partners and to better integrate DOD activities with civilian agencies and organizations. Secretary Gates puts forth the twin agenda of rebalancing and reform as key mechanisms for pursuing this agenda in ways that employ scarce resources effectively and field the necessary U.S. military forces today and tomorrow.

As Secretary Gates's memo makes clear, the QDR Report, along with accompanying budget decisions, aspires to launch DOD on the path of major changes in strategic and military priorities. In particular, it aims at enhancing U.S. military capabilities for waging current conflicts in Iraq, Afghanistan, and elsewhere, while trimming some forces and scaling back expensive modernization programs for the distant future. Such cutbacks are partly motivated by an assessment of strategic requirements, but they also anticipate a future in which DOD budgets will not grow rapidly (if at all), stiff priorities must be met, and painful tradeoffs made. A controversial document, the QDR Report's emphasis on enhancing current warfighting capabilities has gained widespread support in the United States. At the same time, its handling of the future U.S. force structure and modernization plans has attracted stinging criticisms. The result has been a mandate by Congress, supported by Secretary Gates, to instruct a team of outside experts to prepare an Alternative QDR Report that puts forth a different future agenda (discussed below). Past QDR Reports have always triggered debates, but this is the first time that a new QDR Report has provoked an officially sanctioned competitor.

To accomplish its purposes, the QDR Report contains the following sections, which are discussed in sequential order here:

- DOD strategy
- rebalancing the force
- guiding the force posture's evolution
- taking care of DOD people
- strengthening relationships abroad and at home
- reforming how DOD does business.

Defense Strategy. Similar to the NSS 2010, the QDR Report argues that the United States faces a complex and uncertain international security landscape in which the pace of change is accelerating, thereby creating both challenges and opportunities. A key trend, it asserts, is that the distribution of global power is becoming more diffuse in ways that, while make the emerging international system hard to define, will leave the United States as the most powerful actor, but one increasingly obligated to work with allies and partners. As part of this trend, it continues, new powers are rising, nonstate actors are becoming more influential, and proliferation is threatening to spread not only weapons of mass destruction (WMD) but also other destructive technologies. In this setting, the QDR Report claims that the top DOD priority must be to prevail in current operations, especially Afghanistan and Iraq. At the same time, DOD must be mindful of broader trends that are shifting the operational landscape. Such trends, it states, include efforts by potential adversaries—states and nonstate actors alike— to offset U.S. military predominance by shifting to such new methods as hybrid warfare, antiaccess capabilities, and, by some states, long-range and precision weapons intended to contest for control of the land, sea, air, space, and cyberspace domains. Moreover, it claims, failing states and growing radicalism mean that over the coming decades, conflicts are as likely to result from state weakness as from state strength. A major implication, it judges, is that U.S. military forces must remain capable of handling a wide spectrum of future conflicts and missions even as they attend to current conflicts.

To address these global dynamics in a manner that carries out the strategic guidance of the NSS 2010, the QDR Report states that DOD should pursue a defense strategy focused on four priority objectives:

- prevail in today's wars
- prevent and deter conflict
- prepare to defeat adversaries and succeed in a wide range of contingencies
- preserve and enhance the all-volunteer force.

Prevailing in today's wars, the QDR Report states, requires succeeding in Afghanistan and the border regions of Pakistan in ways that defeat al

Qaeda, suppress the Taliban, and strengthen the Afghan government, army, and police force. Success in Afghanistan, it argues, requires not only the ongoing surge of U.S. military forces and partner commitments, but also rapidly increasing the number and quality of such key enablers as air transports and helicopters, unmanned aerial systems, and other combat support/ logistic support assets. In Iraq, the QDR Report envisions the continuing drawdown of U.S. military forces until total withdrawal is completed by late 2011. Elsewhere, it states, the ongoing multitheater fight against al Qaeda and its affiliates will necessitate a U.S. military contribution focused on two basic forms: a highly capable network of special operations and intelligence capabilities, and an enduring effort to build the capacity of key partners around the world.

Preventing and deterring conflict, the QDR Report argues, should focus on existing and potential threats in ways that defend the United States, protect allies, foster regional security, and preserve access to the global commons. While this goal requires multiple instruments and all aspects of national power, it states, DOD can contribute by assisting allies and partners in their defense efforts. It can do so by providing a global defense posture of forward-stationed and deployable forces capable of prevailing across all domains, protecting critical U.S. infrastructure including cyberspace, and sustaining a safe, secure, and effective nuclear arsenal at the lowest levels consistent with U.S. and allied interests. The task of credibly underwriting U.S. commitments while pursuing deterrence, it asserts, requires tailored approaches to deterrence that include an in-depth understanding of the capabilities, intentions, and decisionmaking of adversaries including states and terrorist networks. The United States, it reports, is strengthening its approach to deterrence by three steps. The first is enhancing DOD ability to attribute WMD, space, and cyberspace attacks to hold aggressors responsible and deny them success. The second is closely consulting allies on creating new tailored regional defense architectures that include conventional forces, nuclear forces, and missile defenses. The third is enhancing U.S. and allied resilience—that is, the capacity to recover quickly from attack.

Preparing to defeat adversaries and succeed in a wide range of contingencies, the QDR Report argues, requires that U.S. military forces must provide multiple employment options and capabilities now and in the future. Such options, it states, stretch from supporting a response to an attack or natural disaster at home to defeating al Qaeda and its allies and defeating aggression by adversary states. They also include securing or neutralizing WMD systems in a state that has lost control of them or thwarting a non-state actor that is trying to acquire them, stabilizing failed states that face internal security threats, and preventing human suffering due to genocide or natural disasters abroad. It further states that in the years ahead, DOD must be prepared to prevail in operations that may occur in multiple theaters in overlapping time frames. This includes the capacity to wage war against two capable nation-state aggressors and to carry out other missions in unpredictable combinations. It notes that while recent operations have stressed the ground forces disproportionately, the future operational landscape could portend significant long-duration air and maritime operations for which U.S. military forces must be prepared.

Preserving and enhancing the all-volunteer force, the QDR Report states, mandate attaching higher priority to a goal that for too long has been underemphasized. The long-lasting wars in Iraq and Afghanistan, it points out, have greatly stressed military personnel and their families with repeated deployments. Pursuing an improved situation, it claims, thus requires transitioning to sustainable rotational rates that protect the force's long-term health, even though DOD must remain prepared for periods of significant crises and multiple operations that mandate higher deployment rates, briefer dwell times, and use of the Reserve Component. The QDR Report calls for stronger efforts to address declining retention levels for key personnel and such healthcare problems as increased levels of combat stress, mental health issues, and even suicides. In addition, it states, DOD must expand its Civilian Expeditionary Workforce and spend substantial money on resetting equipment and platforms lost through combat and the strain of today's wars, although not necessarily on a one-for-one basis.

Rebalancing the Force. In the eyes of the QDR Report, rebalancing the force involves pursuing multiple steps aimed at remedying gaps in capabilities in the existing and future posture. It articulates two primary themes: U.S. forces would be better able to perform their missions if they had more and better key enabling capabilities at their disposal (for example, helicopters, unmanned aircraft systems [UAS], intelligence analysis and foreign language expertise, and tactical communication systems); and U.S. forces must be flexible and adaptable, so they can confront the full range of challenges that emerge from the changing international security environment.

By applying available resources wisely, the QDR Report aims at strengthening U.S. military capabilities appreciably in ways that reduce, but not necessarily eliminate, operational and strategic risks. Rebalancing the force, it states, requires investments in six critical mission areas:

- defend the United States and support civilian authorities at home
- succeed in counterinsurgency, stability, and counterterrorism operations
- build the security capacity of partner states
- deter and defeat aggression in antiaccess environments
- prevent proliferation and counter WMD
- operate effectively in cyberspace.

The mission of defending the United States and supporting civilian authorities at home, the QDR Report states, especially requires measures to safeguard against terrorist strikes on the homeland. Accordingly, this mission requires investments in multiple areas:

- field faster, more flexible consequence management assets by increasing the responsiveness of the original chemical, biological, radiological, nuclear, and high-yield explosive Consequence Management Response Force, replacing two other response forces with smaller units focused on command, control, communications assets, and using the National Guard to create 10 Homeland Response Forces
- enhance capabilities for domain awareness by acquiring new technologies

- accelerate the development of standoff radiological detection capabilities by acquiring sensors that will permit better wide-area surveillance at home and abroad
- enhance domestic counter–improvised explosive devices (IED) capabilities by developing better tactics, techniques, and procedures.

The mission of succeeding in counterinsurgency, stability, and counterterrorism operations, the QDR Report states, is not a niche area, but instead requires high-level competencies from all military Services and will remain relevant for the indefinite future. In particular, the report asserts, investments are needed in multiple capabilities that are in high demand and provide key enablers of tactical and operational success:

- increase the availability of rotary-wing assets in the form of more cargo helicopters, naval support helicopters, and two more Army combat aviation brigades
- expand manned and unmanned aircraft systems for intelligence, surveillance, and reconnaissance (ISR) in the form of such long-dwell assets as Predator and Reaper
- expand intelligence, analysis, and targeting capability in the form of more trained manpower and critical support systems
- improve counter-IED capabilities, especially in the form of more and better assets for airborne electronic warfare (EW) currently in high demand
- expand and modernize the AC–130 fleet in the form of modernizing and enlarging the number of AC–130 gunships
- increase key enabling assets for special operations forces (SOF) in the form of more gunships plus more organic combat support and combat service support assets
- increase counterinsurgency, stability, and counterterrorism capacity in the form of additional Army Stryker Brigades, naval riverine assets, and coastal patrol aircraft
- expand Civil Affairs capacity in the form of new Active-duty Civil Affairs brigades and better integration of Civil Affairs activities with

stability operations in Provincial Reconstruction Teams and Human Terrain Teams

- strengthen capabilities for strategic communications in the form of closer collaboration among multiple agencies at all levels, including DOD–Department of State cooperation.

Building the security capacity of partner states, the QDR Report states, is a longstanding but increasingly important mission that is carried out not only by Foreign Military Sales and Foreign Military Financing and officer exchange and education programs; it is also accomplished by new-era security force assistance missions that can involve deployment of sizable U.S. military forces to individual countries to help train, equip, and prepare host-nation forces and defense ministries. Key initiatives of the QDR Report for this mission include:

- strengthen and institutionalize U.S. military capabilities for security force assistance activities in the form of 500 more personnel assigned to trainer-to-trainer units of all four Services, more Air Force Regional Contingency Response Groups, and more Air Force light mobility and light attack aircraft for working with partner air forces

- enhance linguistic, regional, and cultural capacities in the form of additional funds for expanded programs in all three areas

- strengthen and expand capabilities for training partner aviation forces by doubling DOD capacity in this area, including more aircraft for the Air Force 6th Special Operations Squadron

- strengthen capacities for ministerial-level training in the form of expanded programs for providing civilian and military training

- create mechanisms to facilitate rapid transfer of critical materiel by reducing delays and bottlenecks

- strengthen capacities for training regional and international security organizations, including the United Nations and international peace-keeping efforts, along with increased training and education of the forces of participating nations.

The mission of deterring and defeating aggression in antiaccess environments, the QDR Report states, requires paying close attention to new
emerging threats. Gaining access to contested zones, it claims, is critical to
the U.S. strategy of forward defense and power projection in multiple
regions, including the Middle East and Asia. In the past, it argues, this
capacity could often be taken for granted, but in tomorrow's world, this no
longer will be the case because potential adversaries are striving to acquire
military capabilities that, unless countered, could deny access to U.S. forces,
thereby permitting uncontested aggression by them. The QDR Report notes
that North Korea and Iran are acquiring new ballistic missile systems that
could target U.S. forces in ways threatening their sanctuary bases. In addition, it states, the Chinese modernization program is developing and fielding large numbers of medium-range ballistic and cruise missiles, new attack
submarines, long-range air defense systems, electronic warfare assets, satel-
lite attack assets, and cyber attack capabilities. A further menace, it notes,
is that Russia is proliferating modern integrated air defenses, and even such
nonstate actors as Hizballah are acquiring unmanned aerial vehicles and
man-portable air defense systems. Nuclear proliferation, the QDR Report
judges, would gravely enhance threats to U.S. forces, but increasingly strong
conventional capabilities for antiaccess strategies pose significant challenges
of their own. In particular, U.S. air and naval forces could be threatened,
thereby making it harder to project large ground forces to contested areas.

To counter this antiaccess threat, the QDR Report advocates the following set of measures:

- develop a joint air-sea battle concept, now under study by the Air
  Force and Navy, that would enable U.S. forces to work closely together
  in all domains—land, sea, air, space, and cyberspace—to defeat
  antiaccess and area-denial threats

- expand future long-range strike capabilities in the form of enhanced
  assets for U.S. attack submarines, naval UAS systems, Air Force
  bombers, better surveillance, and other improvements to both penetrating platforms and standoff weapons

- exploit advantages in subsurface operations in the form of a new unmanned underwater Navy vehicle

- assure access to space and use of space assets, including use of growing international and commercial expertise, implementation of a 2008 Space Protection Strategy that will reduce vulnerabilities of space systems, and fielding capabilities for rapid augmentation and reconstitution of space capabilities to enhance resilience of space architectures

- defeat enemy sensor and engagement systems in the form of increased investments in capabilities for electronic attack

- enhance the presence and responsiveness of U.S. forces abroad by examining options for deploying and sustaining selective forces in regions facing new challenges, such as home-porting of additional naval forces.

The mission of preventing proliferation and countering weapons of mass destruction, the QDR Report states, is a top national security priority that requires many Federal agencies, with DOD playing a critical role. Portraying WMD proliferation and use as a grave threat with global ramifications, the report points out that WMD systems may fall into the hands of not only hostile states, but also fragile states and ungoverned areas. To counter this trend, it argues, the United States must increase its efforts to detect, interdict, and contain the effects of these weapons. Deterring and defending against such threats, it states, can be enhanced through measures aimed at better understanding them, securing and reducing dangerous materials wherever possible, monitoring and tracking lethal agents, materials, and means of delivery, and, where relevant, defeating the agents themselves.

The QDR Report states that DOD will expand its efforts to counter WMD threats, strengthen interdiction operations, refocus intelligence requirements, strengthen international partnerships, support cooperative threat reduction efforts, and develop countermeasures, defenses, and mitigation strategies. Geographic containment of areas of concern, it continues, will be necessary to ensure that WMD and related materials do not fall into the hands of hostile actors and that effectively responding to WMD-armed threats will require an integrated, layered defense network in multiple regions, as well as the in United States. Such layered defenses are essential, it states, to prevent an attack before it occurs, respond to attack should prevention fail, and help deny state and nonstate adversaries the benefits they seek through threatened or actual use of WMD by raising the costs and risks of such an attack. Accordingly, the QDR Report reveals that DOD will undertake the following steps:

- establish a standing joint task force elimination headquarters to better plan, train, and execute WMD-elimination operations

- research countermeasures and defenses to nontraditional chemical agents in order to create technologies for meeting and defeating these emerging threats

- enhance nuclear forensics to improve the ability to attribute nuclear attacks to their source in ways that enhance deterrence

- secure vulnerable nuclear materials by promoting stringent nuclear security practices for both civilian and military facilities across the globe

- expand the biological threat reduction program to countries outside the former Soviet Union in order to create a global network for surveillance and response

- develop new verification technologies to support a robust arms control, nonproliferation, and counterproliferation agenda.

The mission of operating effectively in cyberspace, the QDR Report states, requires efforts by DOD to protect its vast information networks from cyber attacks from multiple sources by remaining vigilant and prepared to react nearly instantaneously. It reveals that DOD is taking several steps to strengthen its capabilities in cyberspace:

- develop a comprehensive approach to DOD operations in cyberspace in the form of improved cyber defenses in-depth, resilient networks and surety of data, better planning, structures, and relationships, and new operational concepts such as dynamic network defense operations

- develop greater cyberspace expertise and awareness in the form of more cyber experts and greater attention to cyber security
- centralize command of cyberspace operations by standing up U.S. Cyber Command under U.S. Strategic Command
- enhance partnerships with other agencies and governments, including the Department of Homeland Security and international partners.

Guiding the Force Posture's Evolution. Notwithstanding its emphasis on current operations and capabilities, the QDR Report presents material on how the future DOD force posture should be guided, sized, and shaped. Its portrayal of trends for the main force components includes the following:

- U.S. ground forces will remain capable of full-spectrum operations with continued focus on counterinsurgency, stability, and counterterrorist operations
- U.S. naval forces will remain capable of forward presence and power projection operations, while being strengthened by missile defenses and other capabilities
- U.S. air forces will become more survivable as large numbers of fifth-generation aircraft (for example, the Joint Strike Fighter F–35) are added and will acquire greater range, flexibility, and versatility
- SOF capabilities will continue to increase
- across the board, U.S. forces will be improved by acquiring better enabling systems that include ISR, communications networks, base infrastructure, and cyber defenses.

The QDR Report further states that—owing to the DOD assessment of future requirements, budget constraints, and the need to make trade-offs—major cutbacks in procurement programs have been ordered. This step, it claims, reflects an effort to direct scarce resources away from lower priority programs so that more pressing needs can be met and shortfalls remedied. These cutbacks include ending production of the F–22 fighter, restructuring procurement of the DDG–1000 destroyer and the Army's Future Combat Systems, deferring production of maritime prepositioning ships, stretching out procurement of a new class of aircraft carrier, and retirement of aging fourth-generation fighters (for example, F–16s). In addition, it states, DOD is proposing to conclude production of the C–17 transport aircraft, delay the LCC command ship program, cancel the CG(X) cruiser, and terminate the Net Enabled Command and Control program. While acknowledging that these cutbacks will slow the previously planned modernization of U.S. forces, the QDR Report states that DOD will be initiating studies of new operational concepts and examining future capability needs in several areas. These include ISR, fighters and long-range aircraft, joint forcible entry, and information networks and communications.

In addition, the QDR Report puts forth a new force-sizing and force-shaping construct. This construct replaces being prepared for two major regional wars as the main template with a broader approach to carrying out multiple overlapping operations of different types. The QDR Report states that in addition to maintaining ongoing overseas engagement activities, this new construct is anchored in the following combination of scenarios and associated requirements:

- a major stabilization operation, deterring and defeating a highly capable regional aggressor, and dealing with a catastrophic event in the United States
- deterring and defeating two regional aggressors while maintaining a heightened alert posture by other U.S. forces
- a major stabilization operation, a long-duration deterrence operation in a separate theater, a medium-sized counterinsurgency operation, and extended support to civil authorities in the United States.

The QDR Report suggests that while the first cluster of scenarios stresses the force posture's ability to defeat a sophisticated adversary, the second stresses the posture's combined arms capability, and the third stresses forces that perform counterinsurgency, stability, and counterterrorism operations. It envisions that if major regional wars erupt while multiple stabilization and counterinsurgency operations are being carried out, forces can be shifted from the former to the latter. By using this combination of scenarios, the QDR continues, its new force-sizing construct is aimed at supporting the defense strategy's four main goals while helping guide resource allocation decisions in the near and long term. It further states that as DOD transitions into a period of less intensive sustained operations, it will focus more heavily on preparing for a broader and deeper range of prevent-and-deter missions as part of a whole-of-government approach and in concert with allies and partners. Accordingly, it calls for the following force posture during the 2011–2015 period:

- Department of the Army: 73 combat brigades (45 Active and 28 Reserve Component) consisting of a mix of light, Stryker, and heavy Brigade Combat Teams, plus 21 combat aviation brigades, 15 Patriot battalions, and 7 Terminal High Altitude Area Defense batteries

- Department of the Navy: 10 to 11 carriers and 10 carrier air wings, 84 to 88 large surface combatants (including 21 to 32 Aegis missile defense combatants and Aegis ashore), 14 to 28 small surface combatants and 14 mine countermeasure ships, 29 to 31 amphibious warfare ships, 53 to 55 attack submarines, and 4 guided-missile submarines, 126 to 171 ISR and EW aircraft, 98 to 109 support ships, and 3 Marine Expeditionary Forces that include 4 divisions and 4 aircraft wings

- Department of the Air Force: 8 ISR wing-equivalents with 380 primary mission aircraft, 30 to 32 airlift and air-refueling wing-equivalents with 33 aircraft per wing, 10 to 11 theater strike wing-equivalents with 72 aircraft per wing, 5 bomber wings totaling 96 bombers, 6 air superiority wing-equivalents with 72 aircraft per wing, 3 command and control wings, and 10 space and cyberspace wings

- SOF forces: Approximately 600 special operations teams, 3 Ranger battalions, and 165 tilt-rotor and fixed-wing aircraft.

Compared to earlier plans, this posture calls for similar numbers of Army brigades, a similar number of Navy carriers and air wings (but somewhat fewer major combatants and support ships), similar numbers of Air Force bombers, fewer tactical fighter wings that are supplemented by new

ISR wings, and enlarged SOF forces. The overall implication is that compared to now, the future U.S. military posture will be similar in size in many areas, but with somewhat smaller naval and air forces. The QDR Report judges that this posture, enhanced by quality improvements in capabilities, will be adequate to carry out national defense strategy and the new force-sizing construct while providing the necessary flexibility and versatility. But by confining itself to verbal reassurances of adequacy, it does not provide penetrating analysis of the reasons why this future posture will be able to handle the three sets of scenarios, or why the cutbacks in procurement of new platforms and weapons will not unduly retard modernization.

Taking Care of DOD People. Pointing out that years of war have imposed considerable strain on the all-volunteer force, the QDR Report articulates a multipronged program aimed at elevating the priority attached to handling military and civilian personnel. This includes:

- caring for wounded warriors
- managing deployment tempo
- recruiting and retention
- supporting families
- keeping faith with the Reserve Component
- developing future military leaders
- developing the total DOD workforce.

The QDR Report's initiative for improving care of wounded warriors includes a set of measures aimed at enhancing funding and health benefits, establishing Centers of Excellence for treating traumatic injuries, creating a single Disability Evaluation System, improving information-sharing, and upgrading mental health care. The QDR Report's treatment of managing the deployment tempo calls for a goal in which Active military personnel remain 2 years at home for each year abroad, while Reservists spend 5 years at home for each year abroad. Its treatment of recruiting and retention calls for policies aimed at meeting future objectives in both areas, coupled with attracting qualified people and providing more flexible ways for military personnel to transition between Active and Reserve Components. Policies for military family care call for increasing funding by 40 percent in this area, improving DOD schools, phasing out unaccompanied tours in Korea, improving family and community support services, and improving compensation for recovery from catastrophic illnesses.

In addition to highlighting the importance of the Reserve Component posture—National Guard and Reserve forces—in national defense strategy, the QDR Report calls for an improved incentive structure to create easier access to high-demand capabilities, a force-generation model that provides sufficient strategic depth, and a comprehensive study on the future balance between Active and Reserve forces. The QDR Report calls for improvements regarding how the Services generate and sustain their cadres of commissioned and non-commissioned officers. It especially focuses on efforts to improve talents for stability operations, counterinsurgency, and building partner capacities through better foreign language, regional, and cultural skills. In addition, its emphasis on professional military education calls for adequate resources and skilled faculty at DOD schools. Finally, its policies toward the total defense workforce call for proper training of the new Civilian Expeditionary Workforce, common professional training and education for flag officers and civilian senior executives, and a reduction in numbers of private contractors.

Strengthening Relationships Abroad and at Home. Proclaiming that cooperative relationships at home and abroad are key to DOD ability to pursue its strategic goals, the QDR Report puts forth a three-part agenda in this arena:

- strengthen relationships with allies and like-minded partners
- develop the supporting DOD global defense posture
- build close and sustained relationships with U.S. Government agencies and other critical actors at home.

The QDR Report's assessment of policies for improving relationships with allies and partners abroad begins by discussing the transatlantic partnership and the North Atlantic Treaty Organization (NATO), which it portrays as the cornerstone of security and stability in Europe and beyond. It calls upon DOD to work at ensuring a strong Alliance that provides a credible Article 5 security commitment, deters threats to Alliance security, has access to U.S. capabilities such as the phased adaptive approach to European missile defense against proliferation, and takes on such new threats as cyberspace attacks. It further urges NATO to develop its own comprehensive civil-military approach in such places as Afghanistan and to pursue greater cooperation with the European Union. It also calls for increased cooperation with Russia while respecting the sovereignty of Russia's neighbors, and for improved partner relations with Eurasian countries.

In Asia, the QDR Report states that bilateral treaty alliances provide the foundation for U.S. security policies aimed at promoting stability and security. It judges that the emerging security landscape requires a more widely distributed and adaptive U.S. presence that relies upon and better leverages the capabilities of U.S. allies and partners there. In Northeast Asia, it states that DOD is working closely with key allies Japan and South Korea to implement agreed plans and shared visions in order to build a comprehensive alliance of bilateral, regional, and global scope; to realign force postures and restructure allied roles and responsibilities; and to strengthen collective deterrence and defense capabilities. In the Pacific Rim, the QDR Report states that DOD is deepening its partnership with Australia and that, in Southeast Asia, DOD is working closely with longstanding allies Thailand and the Philippines, deepening its partnership with Singapore, and pursuing closer ties with Indonesia. While endorsing a cooperative relationship with China, the QDR Report notes that Chinese military modernization and decisionmaking processes raise legitimate questions about its future conduct and intentions in Asia and beyond. Accordingly, it calls for a U.S. relationship with China that is multidimensional and undergirded by a process that enhances confidence and reduces mistrust in a manner that reflects national interests. In South Asia, the QDR Report calls for close cooperation with India as its military capabilities continue to grow in ways permitting it to be a net provider of security in the Indian Ocean and beyond. It also suggests the further development of a long-term strategic partnership with Pakistan in joint ways that help combat extremism and support its democracy and development.

In the Middle East, the QDR states that regional stability is critical to U.S. interests. Accordingly, it calls for continued close cooperation with Israel as well as growing security partnerships with Egypt, Lebanon, Jordan, Saudi Arabia, Yemen, other Gulf states, and Iraq. These partnerships are aimed at countering emerging threats, including extremism, terrorism, nuclear proliferation, and maritime security challenges. It also proclaims that the United States will work with Middle East partners to develop a regional architecture that broadens and improves interoperable air and missile defenses. In Africa, the QDR Report calls for growing partnerships with key countries and international organizations in ways that help foster stability and prosperity, aid fragile and failed states, and cope with such security challenges as extremism, piracy, and violence. In the Western Hemisphere, the QDR Report states that the United States will work with Canada, Mexico, Brazil, and other partners to address such common problems as narcoterrorist organizations, illicit trafficking, and social unrest.

The QDR Report's assessment of regional policies for maintaining alliances and building partnerships provides a framework for guiding how the global U.S. defense posture should evolve. Noting that large U.S. military forces are deployed abroad for peacetime security-building purposes, it calls for the overseas posture to adapt and evolve in ways that respond to and anticipate changes in the international security environment. Judging that the future will require continuing innovations to meet new challenges, it calls for U.S. military overseas involvements that help foster a new architecture of cooperation. In this way, openings for U.S. forces to work closely with allies and partners can be generated in ways that create efficiencies and synergies from collaborating forces. Accordingly, it calls for a regionally tailored approach to the U.S. military posture that blends forward-stationed and rotationally deployed forces, allows for power projection from the United

States when needed, strengthens assured access to key bases and infrastructure, and provides a stabilizing influence that is welcomed by host nations.

In Europe, the QDR Report calls for a U.S. posture that protects national interests and fulfills NATO commitments, is flexible and deployable, and facilitates multilateral operations inside and outside Europe. Accordingly, it calls for the United States to continue deploying four ground brigades in Europe pending further review, to begin deployment of a revised U.S. missile defense architecture in Europe, and to enhance its forward-deployed naval presence to support improved missile defenses and increase multilateral cooperation on maritime security. In the Pacific, the QDR Report calls for an evolving and adaptive U.S. posture that continues to provide extended deterrence to Japan and Korea and preserves a strong combined U.S.–Republic of Korea defense posture on the peninsula. It also foresees pursuing the bilateral Realignment Roadmap with Japan in ways that retain adequate U.S. force there while transforming Guam into a hub for regional security activities, as well as otherwise promoting enhanced access, cooperative basing, and multilateral military cooperation on new challenges.

In the Greater Middle East and Africa, the QDR Report puts forth broad guidance to sizing and designing the future U.S. military involvement there. It calls upon DOD not only to handle the ongoing involvements in Afghanistan and Iraq, but also to focus on creating a regional strategic architecture that better serves U.S., allied, and partner interests in the medium and long terms. To this end, it calls for enhanced multilateral cooperation with allies and partners and for a reshaped U.S. defense posture that achieves reassurance and deterrence while remaining cognizant of regional sensitivities to a large, long-term U.S. military presence. In Africa, the QDR Report calls for a limited rotating U.S. military presence focused on partnership-building and access to facilities for launching multilateral contingency responses. In the Western Hemisphere, it judges, the United States does not need a robust forward military presence. Instead, it will retain a limited presence that helps foster cooperative multilateral ties and provides capabilities for handling such challenges as control of illicit trafficking, detection and interdiction of WMD, border and coastal security, and humanitarian assistance and disaster relief.

Reforming How DOD Does Business. The QDR Report argues that DOD must reform how it operates internally to provide more agile, innovative, and streamlined processes in five critical areas:

- reforming security assistance
- reforming how weapons are bought
- strengthening the industrial base
- reforming the U.S. export control system
- crafting a strategic approach to climate and energy.

The QDR Report argues that DOD handling of security assistance must be reformed in order to improve how a critical new mission is performed. Whereas during the Cold War, security assistance mainly focused on providing advanced weapons and related assets to close allies and friends, it argues that today it must address how to build defense sectors and pursue reforms in failing states and others requiring such help, many of which fall into the ambiguous gray zone between war and peace. Iraq and Afghanistan, it states, are examples of modern-day security assistance focused on enabling partners to respond to internal and external security challenges. In dealing with this mission, the QDR Report asserts, a whole-of-government approach that produces close interagency collaboration is required, but the DOD role is especially critical. Today's DOD system, it states, is slow and cumbersome, and often results in approaches that start from scratch in each contingency or failure and produces policies limited in scope, duration, and resources. Progress, however, is being made. In addition to gaining approval for recent legislation to strengthen security assistance to Afghanistan and Pakistan, the QDR Report states, the administration has launched a comprehensive review of security sector assistance. Meanwhile, DOD is striving to increase its skilled manpower in this area, meet urgent warfighter needs, and establish a fund that would allow it to maintain an inventory of items commonly needed by partners.

The QDR Report emphasizes that pursuing reforms in how DOD acquires new weapons and other costly assets is a key goal. Today, it says, the DOD acquisition process is encumbered by a small set of expensive weapons programs with unrealistic requirements, cost and schedule over-runs, and unacceptable performance. Four key problems arise:

- requirements for new systems are often set at the far end of techno-logical boundaries
- the acquisition workforce has been allowed to atrophy, including in critical skills
- the approach to defining requirements and developing capabilities too often relies on overly optimistic cost estimates
- delivery of logistical support to field commanders suffers from inefficiencies.

To help overcome these problems, the QDR Report states, the Weapon Systems Acquisition Reform Act was signed into law in 2009 with the goal of limiting cost overruns before they spiral out of control, and of improving oversight of major weapon system programs. In addition, it reports, DOD is taking steps to develop a larger cadre of trained acquisition professionals. Beyond this, it states, DOD will strive to ensure that requirements for all new major weapons are subjected to careful analysis and to certify that new tech-nologies are sufficiently mature before the final costly phase of engineering and manufacturing development is launched. Additional DOD reforms, it continues, include steps to improve cost analysis. They also include means to improve program execution by employing fixed-price development contracts, constraining the tendency to add requirements to programs, creating com-petitive prototypes early in the research, development, test, and evaluation cycle, certifying technology maturity through independent reviews, conduct-ing realistic testing to identify problems as early as possible, demanding sound performance from contractors, and avoiding sacrifices to costs and schedules for promises of improved performance. Finally, the QDR Report calls for steps to institutionalize a rapid, agile acquisition capability for speeding delivery of new systems and weapons when they are needed and to launch an effort to control DOD's rising costs for health care.

The QDR Report's treatment of measures to strengthen the industrial base calls for market-based efforts to lessen reliance on a few big contractors by working with the entire spectrum of defense firms, purely commercial firms, and other technologically advanced firms and institutions. Its approach to reforming the U.S. export control system claims that today, this system is complicated by too many redundancies, tries to protect too much, and poses a risk to national security in ways that mandate fundamental reform. It calls for steps aimed at lessening redundancies, roadblocks, and constraints while improving cooperation, technology-sharing, and interoperability with allies and partners. An overall goal is to strengthen controls on new technologies that need protecting, to speed delivery of weapons and other systems that should be made available abroad, and to encourage greater collaboration between U.S. and foreign industries. Its approach to climate and energy calls for greater DOD attention to both arenas in ways that increase use of renewable energy supplies, reduce energy demand and greenhouse gas emissions, and make domestic facilities more efficient.

Strengths, Shortfalls, and Lingering Issues. By any measure, the QDR Report is a large and comprehensive document, much larger than previous QDR Reports issued over the past 15 years. Compared to those documents, it includes traditional material, but unlike them, it includes considerable material on new issues. Accordingly, it illuminates the extent to which the U.S. defense enterprise has become more complex and demanding in recent years. During the 1990s, the end of the Cold War in Europe and victory in Operation *Desert Storm* enabled DOD to focus mainly on preparing its military forces for traditional major regional wars, such as against North Korea. Beginning in late 2001, events compelled DOD not only to consider hypothetical regional wars, but also to launch a global war against terror and to invade both Afghanistan and Iraq. Simultaneously, DOD launched a major transformation agenda aimed at configuring its military forces with new information networks and other systems to wage the high-tech wars of the future.

Looking back from the standpoint of today, even that demanding agenda seems relatively straightforward and simple. As the QDR Report makes clear, DOD must not only handle traditional missions but also carry out demanding stability operations in Afghanistan and Iraq, build security partnerships with internally troubled states, work with other U.S. agencies, attend to new homeland security and cyber defense challenges, and improve U.S. military forces for the long term with investment budgets that present significant shortfalls in available resources. Whether the QDR Report adequately addresses all of these challenges is debated by some critics, but regardless of how it is appraised, it does successfully illuminate the very complex challenges and thorny issues facing DOD today and tomorrow.

The QDR Report is complementary to the NSS 2010 in ways intended to harmonize U.S. national security strategy and defense planning, and it aptly discusses many defense issues that are not addressed by the NSS 2010. Similar to the NSS 2010, it is best evaluated not by how it handles a plethora of details, but by whether it judges the strategic and military basics correctly. A mixed appraisal seems appropriate because the QDR Report has many strengths but, in the eyes of critics at least, some shortfalls as well.

A main strength of the QDR Report is that it puts forth an overall U.S. defense strategy with four organizing concepts of prevail, prevent, prepare, and preserve. As it makes clear, prevailing in today's wars is top priority. Simultaneously, DOD must prevent and deter other conflicts and damaging trends, while preparing to defeat future adversaries and succeed in a wide range of operations and preserving the all-volunteer force. In addition, the QDR Report encapsulates DOD's emerging activities in two action-oriented terms: rebalance and reform. Whereas *rebalance* refers to how the force structure is to be strengthened now and in the future, *reform* mainly refers to how DOD acquisition process and security assistance efforts are to be improved to overcome their sluggish performance. By mating its four-pronged defense strategy with its two-pronged approach to change, the

QDR Report broadly illustrates the strategic agenda that DOD will be pursuing in the coming years.

The QDR Report devotes little discussion to how future defense budgets—which probably will not continue benefiting from major real growth—will unfold. But since its publication, Defense Secretary Robert Gates has made clear that stiff priorities will have to be set and some activities scaled back so that scarce funds can be saved and investment funds increased. As Secretary Gates pointed out, peacetime DOD budgets have grown by about 40 percent in real terms since 2001, but much of the increase has been consumed by rising costs for personnel and operations, thereby constraining growth of investment and procurement budgets. In 2009, Secretary Gates slashed several major programs for acquiring new weapons, thereby saving about $350 billion over 10 years and bringing out-year procurement spending into alignment with budget realities. In 2010, he announced a plan to shift about 6 percent of DOD's budget from low-priority programs to high-priority ones, as well as steps to close U.S. Joint Forces Command and other staffs while trimming senior civilian and military posts and civilian contractors.

Meanwhile, Secretary Gates asked Congress to fund 1 percent annual real increases to DOD budgets in the coming years. His actions have been controversial in some quarters, but they are designed to harness the DOD budget to support the QDR Report's assessment of future defense strategy, rebalance, and reform. Secretary Gates's call for DOD to find $100 billion in savings that could be reprogrammed was successful. It resulted in $70 billion to be reinvested in the procurement accounts of all Services, and the additional savings to be spent on health care and other measures. As of early 2011, official forecasts were suggesting that the DOD budget would benefit from little real growth through 2011. Projected defense budget cuts of about $78 billion through 2015 evidently will require manpower reductions of 27,000 to the Army and 15,000 to 20,000 to the Marine Corps, plus trimming of some procurement programs. Larger spending cuts—for example, up to $400 billion in reductions over the next 10 years—will require even deeper pairing of defense manpower, force structures, and improvement programs in ways that will mandate further reviews of U.S. military roles, missions, and responsibilities.

Another strength of the QDR Report is its handling of the rebalancing agenda by focusing on six key military missions that range from succeeding in current conflicts and helping partner states to strengthening U.S. forces for antiaccess operations, preventing WMD proliferation, and improving homeland security and cyberspace defenses. In addressing these six missions, the QDR Report puts forth 35 separate improvement programs and measures, all of which are intended to elevate U.S. military capabilities in their respective areas. The mission of succeeding in counterinsurgency, stability, and counterterrorism operations—a clear near-term priority—receives special attention, with nine improvement programs designed mainly to enhance ground force operations. The mission of developing better capabilities for operating in antiaccess environments—a longer term priority— also is noteworthy because it contains six measures that are mainly focused on enhancing naval and air forces against future threats that could be posed by such well-armed adversaries as China. A clear implication is that additional funds should be spent in these 35 areas in ways that impinge upon funds for other investments. Even so, the QDR Report seems correct in judging that if U.S. military forces improve in these six areas, they will be better prepared for challenges ahead.

Yet another strength is the QDR Report's treatment of how to bolster relationships at home and abroad by working closely with the militaries of allies and partners in key regions, deploying missile defenses as part of new regional deterrence architectures, and making improvements to U.S. forces and operations overseas. In this arena, the QDR Report helps close a gap in the NSS 2010, which did not devote adequate attention to regional security priorities other than the Middle East. In doing so, however, the QDR Report only addresses military issues, not underlying political design concepts. A final strength of the QDR Report is its handling of reforms to how DOD does business. In particular, its focus on pursuing reforms to weapons acquisition addresses a longstanding problem that, over the years, has produced too many overly costly weapons well after they were needed. Whether the QDR Report's reforms will be fully acted upon remains to be seen, but they are pointed in the right direction.

A key shortcoming of the QDR Report, as critics have alleged, is a lackluster handling of policies and plans for guiding the future evolution of U.S. military forces. The QDR Report takes a step in the right direction by replacing the old template of two regional wars with a new force-sizing construct of three different scenario clusters. These reflect shifting combinations of stabilization operations, deterrence and defeat of two regional aggressors, long-enduring deterrence operations, and catastrophic events in the United States. Indeed, future U.S. military forces would have impressive capabilities if they were sufficiently large, diverse, and versatile to meet requirements for all three clusters. But will this be the case?

The QDR Report fails to address, much less answer, this question; it provides clarity about how the future force posture will take shape, but offers no metrics or penetrating analysis of whether and how this posture will meet these clusters of requirements or of risks and insufficiencies that might arise. This issue is more than academic. The United States currently has the best military in the world, but recent years have shown that it is often stretched thin by deployment operations and requirements in multiple theaters. Whether it can handle two concurrent regional wars has long been debated, and the new force-sizing construct seems to elevate requirements, not diminish them. The problem is that, in naval and air forces, tomorrow's posture will be smaller than today's. Will quality improvements offset potential shortages in numbers? Perhaps so, but the QDR Report does not reveal why this will be the case.

Another shortfall is the QDR Report's failure to discuss the importance of joint operations and how they can be improved. For the past decade and longer, strengthening the capacity for joint operations that involve land, sea, and air components has been a main goal of DOD and the military Services. While progress has been made, perfection is far from achieved. Instead of highlighting the need for further progress, the QDR Report discusses the ground, naval, and air forces separately, largely in isolation from each other rather than in a joint context. The one exception is its endorsement of a new air-sea battle concept for dealing with antiaccess threats, but currently this is an idea under study, not a tangible program for acquiring new capabilities. Otherwise, the QDR Report offers assurances that all Services will be strengthened, but at times, its interpretation suggests a future bifurcated posture. Thus, ground forces will handle gritty conflicts in the Middle East while naval and air forces mainly focus on deterring powerful countries such as China. Perhaps a bifurcated posture reflects a natural evolutionary trend that responds to current events, but is it safe to assume that future conflicts will not require a close fusion of all three components? The QDR Report is silent on this question, but it needs an answer because future plausible wars with such countries as North Korea, Iran, and Russia could be hard to win in absence of one component or another.

A final shortfall comes from how the QDR Report handles future force modernization for the long haul. For most of the past decade, a main DOD clarion call for improving force capabilities has been transformation—the 20-year process by which U.S. military forces are not only to be modernized with new weapons but also to acquire new information networks, munitions, doctrines, practices, and other assets in order to be prepared for a future in which technologies and operational concepts will be different from the past. The QDR Report does not even mention the word *transformation*, much less describe its future course. Nor does it offer any replacement term or concept for guiding DOD in the years ahead. Nor does it address a more fundamental issue: the degree to which future U.S. forces are expected to retain their current qualitative superiority over adversary forces, which themselves will be improving. In principle, a U.S. defense strategy that relies on somewhat smaller forces to perform a broad spectrum of missions and to wage war against improved adversary forces would seem to place a high premium on preserving or enhancing qualitative superiority. The QDR Report seemingly shares this approach in its discussion of strategy principles.

Yet it does not reveal in any depth how this approach is being applied in concrete terms and whether it can be expected to succeed.

Beyond this, the QDR Report neglects to provide guidance on how specific modernization plans and programs—key engines for replacing aging inventories and building better capabilities—are to unfold. What it offers instead is a discussion of the many new weapons that have been cancelled or scaled back, some because they seemed gold-plated or low priority, but others because they could not be afforded in an era of overloaded procurement budgets. A main impact is that the Army, Navy, and Air Force have been stripped of several new weapons that they regarded as cornerstones of their modernization—for example, new Army combat vehicles, Navy cruisers and destroyers, and Air Force F–22 fighters and cargo planes. In some cases, replacement weapons and systems are being pursued. For example, the Air Force will benefit from large numbers of F–35 fighters, unmanned aerial system (UAS) aircraft, and deep-strike assets that will help offset loss of more F–22 fighters. But although the QDR Report proclaims that the Army and Navy will remain capable of carrying out their missions, it leaves the fate of their modernization plans unclear. Indeed, the QDR Report does not even provide the standard feature of most past QDR Reports and Secretary of Defense posture statements: a comprehensive list of major modernization plans that will be pursued by all four Services. As a result, the QDR Report fails to provide assurance, much less analysis, that when remaining, still-funded modernization programs are added up, they will produce an adequately equipped U.S. military posture 10 years from now. In this arena, the QDR Report seems so preoccupied with handling near-term imperatives that it largely produces an analytical void on where the distant future should be headed.

CHAPTER THREE

The QDR in Perspective: Meeting America's National Security Needs in the 21st Century

D
issatisfaction with the Quadrennial Defense Review (QDR) Report's alleged near-term, "business as usual" focus as well as other perceived shortcomings led Congress, supported by Defense Secretary Robert Gates, to mandate preparation of an alternative QDR Report by a panel of 20 independent civilian and military experts led by Stephen Hadley and William Perry. Written to provide a broader, longer term perspective, the resulting 132-page study issued in late July 2010 is more alarmist than the QDR Report. Warning of an impending "train wreck" ahead for the Department of Defense (DOD), it puts forth numerous recommendations aimed at correcting the problems facing DOD and the U.S. Government in pursuing national security strategy and defense planning. Some of its recommendations accelerate changes already endorsed by the QDR Report, but others pursue new directions. The result is a useful complement to the QDR Report, but not a wholesale replacement of it. The two studies are best appraised in the context of each other in order to identify similarities and differences.

In crafting a broad strategic approach, *The QDR in Perspective: Meeting America's National Security Needs in the 21st Century* (QDRP Report) identifies four enduring national interests that will continue to animate U.S. defense policy: homeland defense; assured access to the sea, airspace, and cyberspace commons; preservation of a favorable balance of power across Eurasia that prevents authoritarian domination of that region; and provision for the global common good through humanitarian aid, developmental assistance, and disaster relief. It also identifies the five grave threats likely to arise to those interests over the next generation:

- radical Islamic extremism and terrorism
- competition from rising global powers in Asia
- continuing struggle for power in the Persian Gulf and the Middle East
- accelerating global competition for resources
- persistent problems from failed and failing states.

This combination of U.S. interests and dangerous threats leads the QDRP Report to conclude that there will be an increased demand on U.S. "hard power" to preserve regional balances in ways mandating that security concerns will remain quite important. In addition, it states that the various tools of "soft power"—for example, diplomacy, trade, and communications—will be increasingly important. The need to apply both hard power and soft power leads the QDRP Report to conclude that the United States must retain its global leadership role while improving its own assets and working to strengthen allies, partners, and international institutions that can contribute to security and peace.

The result is a framework that basically endorses the QDR Report's four strategy concepts and six high priority mission areas, but urges a more galvanized and energetic set of activities to increase DOD and U.S. Government capabilities for the long haul. In surveying DOD and the government, the QDRP Report warns of an impending train wreck in military personnel, acquisitions, and force structure coming from aging equipment inventories, declining size of the Navy, escalating personnel entitlements, and growing stress on U.S. military forces. To address these and other problems, the QDRP Report advances an integrated set of key recommendations:

- build an alternative force structure with emphasis on increasing the size of the Navy
- modernize the equipment inventories of all Services

- increase DOD capability to contribute to homeland defense and handle such asymmetric threats as cyber attack
- improve DOD personnel policies in ways that strengthen the all-volunteer force
- vigorously reform the DOD acquisition process
- foster whole-of-government and comprehensive approaches and better civilian capacity in order to develop better soft power for national security challenges
- create a new, comprehensive strategic planning process for national security that provides better management, more holistic planning, and improved crisis response.

Building an Alternative, Modernized Force Structure. Focused on ensuring that the U.S. military posture is adequately large and configured to handle threats and perform missions 10 or more years from now, the QDRP Report is sharply critical of the QDR Report's force-sizing construct. The latter allegedly lacks clarity and analytical insight on the relationship between future requirements and force capabilities. In the absence of an adequate force-sizing construct, the QDRP Report calls for a return to the baseline force structure adopted by the Bottom-Up Review of 1993, which was designed to fight two concurrent regional wars. It accepts that U.S. ground forces will remain largely focused on Middle East operations for the foreseeable future, but it wants to ensure that naval and air forces are adequate for future missions in other theaters.

The QDRP Report does not propose major increases to the Army and Air Force postures, but it does endorse expansion of the Navy from 288–322 ships to 346 ships. A key goal, it states, is to increase the U.S. military force structure in the Asia-Pacific region in ways largely anchored in a maritime strategy. Worried about China's rise and a decline of U.S. influence that could undermine existing treaty obligations, it emphasizes forward naval power there in ways that seemingly tilt away from the QDR Report's partial shift to a standoff strategy focused on long-range strike assets. It supports the emerging DOD attempt to develop a new air-sea battle concept, which seems especially relevant to the Asia-Pacific region. The QDRP Report also calls for parallel increases in force structure in ways that counter antiaccess and area-denial challenges, strengthen homeland and cyberspace defense, and enhance assets for postconflict stabilization missions.

The QDRP Report is particularly intent on urging a faster, more ambitious pace for recapitalizing and modernizing the U.S. military's aging inventories of major weapons and other equipment. Background information here is essential to understanding the differing approaches of the QDR Report and QDRP Report in this critical arena. The governing reality is that many U.S. military weapons for waging major combat operations were procured during the 1980s and 1990s. The Services began developing new weapons to replace them some years ago, but owing to the focus on Iraq and Afghanistan and other constraints, they progressed slowly through the research, development, test, and evaluation (RDT&E) cycle during 2000–2009. As the new decade dawned, the Services had planned to use growing acquisition budgets after 2010 to hasten the development of new tanks, ships, and fighter aircraft, and then to procure them in large numbers over the following years.

Recognizing that these new weapons would cost more than envisioned procurement budgets allowed and doubting the need for some of them, Secretary Gates in 2009 announced his decision to cancel or scale back many of these programs. The new Air Force F–35 Joint Strike Fighter (JSF) fighter survived the chopping block, but the F–22 fell victim as did much of the Army's Future Combat System program and the Navy's plans to acquire new combat ships. Whereas the QDR Report ratified this choice, the QDRP Report questions its wisdom because, in a few years, it allegedly would leave the Services with too many aging weapons that ultimately will be unable to perform new missions and counter new threats.

Accordingly, the QDRP Report calls for the spigots of modernization to be reopened over the coming decade. It states that the U.S. military should be allowed to acquire a new generation of armored vehicles, warships, fighter aircraft, sensors, munitions, and other weapons to refresh aging inventories, maintain an adequately large posture, and preserve the qualitative supremacy of U.S. forces over adversaries. In addition, it states, modernization would add necessary new capabilities in such areas as defeating antiaccess and area-denial threats, improving deep-strike assets, strengthening forward presence and power projection, and offsetting adversary acquisition of modern air defenses and precision-strike munitions. In this arena, the QDRP Report is pointing to a significantly bigger and faster modernization than envisioned by the QDR Report. It judges that this robust modernization program cannot be fully funded by projected DOD investment budgets or even with the reprioritized RDT&E and procurement funds being sought by Secretary Gates. Accordingly, it calls for significant, enduring increases to DOD investment spending that would elevate current procurement budgets well above today's level of $120 billion, and keep them there for the next decade and beyond. The QDRP Report does not say whether this extra spending is to come from elsewhere in the DOD budget or from additional congressional appropriations, but it does call for using technology to drive down the costs of new weapons so that both adequate quantity and quality can be afforded.

Strengthening Homeland Defense and Cyberspace Defense. In both of these arenas, the QDRP Report offers judgments similar to those of the QDR Report, but expresses them in more graphic ways. The QDRP Report expresses concern that during a period of ongoing contingency operations abroad, the U.S. military will lack the assets to perform an expansive homeland defense mission on short notice. It worries about a natural disaster, but a main concern is the prospect of a weapon of mass destruction (WMD) detonation on U.S. soil that could cause immense damage. In such a situation, it judges, DOD would transition from supporting the Department of Homeland Security to taking charge. DOD, it states, needs proper legal authorities to carry out this role, and it should take steps to ensure that a portion of the National Guard can be quickly mobilized to contribute. In addressing cyberspace, the QDRP Report judges that cyber threats are increasing in ways that menace DOD information networks as well as national infrastructure. It calls for DOD to be able to defend its networks at home and abroad from attack. However, it also states that DOD should possess the capacity to shut down attacks instantaneously at the point of origin as part of a larger government effort to identify the types of cyber attacks that should be treated diplomatically as acts of war and to eliminate them. The QDRP Report calls for major increases in the resources committed to cyberspace security. Similar to the QDR Report, it applauds creation of U.S. Cyber Command, but it notes that a larger cadre of trained cyberspace professionals will be needed.

Strengthening the All-Volunteer Force. In this arena, the QDRP Report puts forth judgments similar to those of the QDR Report, but offers a broader, more penetrating set of improvement measures. The QDRP Report proclaims that recent and dramatic growth in the cost of the all-volunteer force cannot be sustained for the long term. Failure to address costs, it states, likely will result in a reduction of the force structure, fewer benefits, or less qualified personnel. Accordingly, it recommends major changes to the military personnel system. These include greater differences in assignment and compensation between one or two terms of service and a career, increased cash-in-hand for those serving less than an entire career, and use of bonuses and credits to reward critical specialties and outstanding performance. They also include a continuum-of-service model that allows Servicemembers to move fluidly between the Active and Reserve Components and among the military, private sector, civil service, and other employment. Beyond this, the QDRP Report states that current limitations on length of service provide insufficient time for personnel to gain the education, training, and experience needed for 21st-century warfare. It recommends lengthening military career opportunities to 40 years, broadening educational opportunities, and making military health care more affordable. It calls for establishing a new National Commission on Military Personnel to develop its recommendations and build support for them.

The QDRP Report also calls for improvements to professional military education (PME). It calls for offering full college scholarships on a competitive basis in exchange for 5 years of Active service as an officer. It calls for Service academies and Reserve Officers' Training Corps programs to offer better education on military affairs and related social sciences. It calls for programs that offer early career officers the opportunity to attend graduate schools to study military affairs or foreign languages and cultures and that mandate a graduate degree for all officers promoted to the rank of lieutenant colonel/commander or above. Calling for efforts to improve the quality of intermediate and senior Service schools, it states that service on a PME teaching faculty should be a requirement for promotion to flag rank, and it continues that PME educational curricula need to be given adequate depth and rigor to better motivate attendees. To upgrade the influence of PME in DOD, it calls for creating a Pentagon Chief Learning Officer at the Assistant Secretary level and for assigning a senior flag officer to be chancellor for all PME schools.

Reforming the DOD Acquisition Process. The QDRP Report looks favorably upon the QDR Report's treatment of the need to reform the DOD acquisition process for developing and buying new weapons and other systems. Nonetheless, it judges that the QDR Report did not go far enough in identifying root causes or proposing effective reforms. Similar to the QDR Report, the QDRP Report laments the well documented failures of the acquisition process, including lengthy delays in producing new weapons, failure to respond to urgent needs of combatant commanders, inflated requirements for new technology, lack of competition, and cost overruns. The fundamental reason for this poor performance, it states, is fragmentation of authority and responsibility for managing acquisition efforts. Such fragmentation, it argues, exists at all levels of the acquisition process, from identifying needs and defining alternative solutions to choosing and resourcing acquisition programs and delivering them on schedule at acceptable cost. This problem, it states, begins from the moment that a new weapon is approved by the Joint Requirements Oversight Committee. It becomes therefore a program of record that is treated as nearly immortal regardless of subsequent delays and cost overruns. Performance, it states, is rarely traded off, and only in the most egregious cases are flawed programs cancelled; too often, success is achieved only with the personal intervention of the Office of the Secretary of Defense (OSD) and that of other senior DOD leaders.

To solve these problems, the QDRP Report urges a strong effort to vest authority and responsibility on individuals in positions of line management so that better program management is brought to bear on all major projects. With proper managerial authority and responsibility, it judges, relevant capabilities for current operational needs (for example, needs in Afghanistan) can be delivered within weeks or months, and major new weapons systems can be fielded within 5 to 7 years, not the 10 to 15 years often taken now. Part of the reason for long delays, it claims, is that development projects (for instance, the F–22) typically try to produce major leaps in technology and performance in a single step.

A better model, it judges, is a development process that provides a service-able weapon within 5 to 7 years—a good time frame for judging achievable technology—and then makes incremental improvements as subsequent models are produced. A good example is the F–16 program, which produced a good fighter in a few years and then subsequently improved it with better capabilities as new models were produced over 20 to 30 years. Recognizing that some programs nonetheless will face challenges, the QDRP Report states, tradeoffs in schedule, cost, or performance may have to be made. It reasons that while often the best model will be adhering to original costs and schedules and accepting less performance, tradeoffs in performance can be judged credibly only by force providers—another good reason for vesting authority and responsibility for program management in the military Services and defense agencies with proper OSD oversight. In addition, the QDRP Report urges greater competition among dual sources before final decisions to develop and procure new weapons are made—a strategy that was employed in a host of successful weapons development programs. Dual-source compe-tition, it states, will require DOD to reverse its current reliance on a small number of large defense industries by returning to a model of more defense contractors and greater competition among them.

Accordingly, the QDRP Report puts forth a set of recommendations:

- The Secretary of Defense should establish lead acquisition roles in a manner that assigns responsibility for identifying gaps in capabilities and executable solutions to force providers (for example, combatant commanders, Services, and defense agencies), uses OSD and Joint Staff to make decisions about choosing and resourcing solutions, and employs the lead Service/agency to deliver new weapons on schedule and within cost estimates.

- For each program, an unbroken chain of command should be established within the force provider community, one that runs from senior OSD authorities to the relevant Service secretary/defense agency, then to the Program Executive Officer, program manager, and defense contractor.

- When urgent needs arise, adjustments should be made in the formal process to deliver effective products within a period of weeks or months, rather than years.

- OSD should return to dual-source competition rather than single-source contracting.

Fostering Improved Whole-of-government Activities, Comprehensive Approaches, and Civilian Capacities. Many future national security challenges, the QDRP Report states, will require an adroit blending of hard power and soft power. For example, the ongoing operation in Afghanistan and efforts to help failing states necessitate a mix of military forces to suppress violence and build host-nation security forces, coupled with civilian assets to promote good governance and economic development. To address this need in ways similar to the QDR Report, the QDRP Report calls for better capacities to pursue whole-of-government approaches and comprehensive approaches. It defines *whole of government* as efforts to merge multiple departments and agencies into a coherent enterprise and *comprehensive approaches* as efforts to coordinate U.S. activities with host nations, allies and partner nations, and international organizations. In addition to pursuing progress in both areas, the QDRP Report calls for creating greater civilian capacities for carrying out future political-military operations in key regions.

Arguing that the U.S. Government does not currently do a good job of handling whole-of-government and comprehensive approaches, the QDRP Report calls for measures aimed at fostering improved interagency planning and coordination among DOD, State Department, Intelligence Community, and other agencies. It also calls for a rebalancing of military and civilian capabilities in ways aimed at lessening demands on the U.S. military in stability and reconstruction missions by increasing the cadre of civilians in DOD, State Department, and other agencies that are trained for deployment missions. In addition, it calls for better management of contractors and reforms to expand the scope and flexibility of U.S. security assistance policies. Such goals lead the QDRP Report to put forth the following recommendations:

- Congress should pursue several legislative steps aimed at reforming the national security effort, such as restructuring Titles 10, 22, 32, and 50 in order to enhance interagency cooperation while clarifying roles and responsibilities for departments and agencies, strengthening educational programs, and creating interagency teams that plan and exercise for future deployments.

- The executive branch should establish a consolidated budget line for national security that, at a minimum, includes DOD, State, U.S. Agency for International Development (USAID), and the Intelligence Community; the Office of Management and Budget should develop a mechanism to track implementation of whole-of-government and comprehensive approaches.

- Congress and the President should establish a National Commission on Building the Civil Force in ways aimed at increasing U.S. civilian capacities in multiple departments and agencies.

- DOD, State, and other agencies should strengthen capacities for pursuing overseas missions and comprehensive approaches.

- The U.S. Government should aspire to reform international security and assistance efforts in ways aimed at strengthening comprehensive approach capacities of allies and partners.

Creating a New Strategic Planning Process for National Security. The QDRP Report concludes with a section that is critical of the QDR Report. Specifically, the QDR Report demonstrates an alleged lack of strategic guidance for the next 20 years, its domination by staffs that handle narrow program and budget issues in parochial ways, its failure to put forth a better DOD force structure and modernization plan for the long term, and its lack of vision and innovation. Such problems lead the QDRP Report to conclude that in coming years, the entire QDR process should be scrapped because, presumably, it is beyond salvation. The QDRP Report calls upon DOD to rely on its normal Planning, Programming, Budgeting, and Execution System (PPBES) to perform functions now handled by the QDR Report. To help foster new and better strategic planning across the government and the interagency community, the QDRP Report recommends the following steps:

- Congress and the executive branch should establish an Independent Strategic Review Panel of outside experts that would convene every 4 years, at the time a new administration is inaugurated, to assess the international environment and recommend changes to existing national security strategy.

- Once this panel has issued its findings, the National Security Council staff would employ them to craft a "grand strategy" that would be formalized as the new National Security Strategy reflecting the President's views and priorities.

- This new strategy would drive subsequent strategic reviews by key executive branch departments, including DOD, State/USAID, Homeland Security, and Intelligence Community, all of which would be animated by the goals of supporting the new National Security Strategy, integrating departmental reviews with it, and identifying mission critical elements.

- The National Security Advisor will be responsible for guiding and coordinating subsequent strategy implementation by participating departments and agencies.

Strengths, Shortfalls, and Lingering Issues. The QDRP Report effort was launched because the QDR Report left critics dissatisfied with its strategic reasoning and force enhancement proposals. When it was published, the QDRP Report echoed these criticisms, but careful appraisal of its content suggests that is best seen as a complement to the QDR Report rather than a competitor or a replacement for it. Both documents have important strengths, but in differing ways. Whereas the QDR Report does a good job of focusing attention on enhancing DOD capabilities for current and near-term operations, the QDRP Report does a good job of addressing long-term goals and priorities. Both perspectives are valuable. Together they crystallize a critical issue: How much emphasis should be placed on preparedness for near-term operations versus different long-term priorities, and how should a proper balance be struck between them? The two studies answer this question in different ways, but a fully satisfactory judgment can be formed only by referencing both studies, rather than one in absence of the other. For this reason, the two studies feed off each other in ways that are constructively interactive, not mutually exclusive.

Notwithstanding their differences, the two documents are similar in how they address strategic affairs. Both are global in scope, focus heavily on the Middle East and Asia, and warn of troubles and threats ahead such as terrorism, WMD proliferation, rival adversaries, and potential conflicts. Although the QDRP Report talks in more overt geopolitical terms than the more muted QDR Report, they are similar in the ways they endorse national security strategies, goals, and missions; handle Iraq and Afghanistan; and treat foreign countries (allies, partners, neutral big powers, and adversaries). In handling these strategic affairs, the QDRP Report is more concerned with future management challenges facing DOD and the U.S. Government, and more vocal about calls for reforms, but the QDR Report acknowledges these challenges and advocates its own case for reforms and rebalancing. Both studies agree that in future years, DOD will need to show greater skill at applying its resources because defense budgets will no longer be growing rapidly.

In addressing specific issues, many similarities abound. Both studies call for improvements in U.S. military forces and the all-volunteer force, better homeland security and cyberspace defense, stronger whole-of-government and comprehensive approaches, better interagency coordination, and close working relationships with partners abroad. They both call for enhanced civilian capacities for future operations requiring them, as well as for close civilian-military coordination and cooperation in the field. Both call for reforms to DOD's troubled, slow, and expensive acquisition process to do a better job of producing new weapons and other systems in ways that are faster, cheaper, and more effective. The QDRP Report does a better job of probing root causes for difficulties facing the acquisition process as well as basic management reforms needed to rectify matters, but both studies are advocating ways to achieve the same positive results. Conversely, the QDR Report does a better job of discussing reforms to security assistance, but again, both studies are pushing in the same strategic directions. Because each study often provides a detailed treatment of issues not addressed heavily by the other, together the two studies do well at covering the waterfront even though both suffer from the drawback of not addressing in enough depth DOD/government future budgets and spending patterns.

The QDRP Report is critical of the QDR Report for not proposing a better force-sizing construct and for not identifying a better U.S. military posture for the long haul. But the QDRP Report proposes no force-sizing construct of its own—and in reasoning that the 1993-approved posture makes sense for the future, it quarrels with the QDR Report only by proposing an enlargement of the Navy beyond approved levels. More naval combatants may make sense because of emerging requirements in Asia, but otherwise, the QDRP Report proposes future ground and air forces that differ little from the QDR Report. The QDRP Report differs appreciably with the QDR Report in its call for a faster, more ambitious force modernization of U.S. ground, naval, and air forces. This recommendation has strategic logic on its side, but in order to carry it out, larger acquisition budgets are needed. The QDR Report's allegedly lackluster treatment of modernization priorities derives partly from awareness that future acquisition budgets likely will not be large enough to fund all of the many desirable weapons and other programs. The QDRP Report opens the door to additional modernization, but because it does not identify where the necessary funds are to come from, it either risks breaking the bank or fails to be clear about where sacrifices must be made elsewhere.

Where does sound policy for modernization lie? Perhaps somewhere between these two perspectives, but identifying a proper path ahead requires a penetrating treatment of future modernization programs and budgets in ways that neither document provides. Because future defense budgets will not be growing in major real terms, much depends upon whether they can be squeezed in ways that channel more funds into procurement and modernization. Part of today's budgetary challenge stems from a multiyear trend that has seen expenses for personnel, peacetime operations, and health care soar. The result has been slower growth in investment spending than otherwise would have been the case. In mid-2010, Secretary Gates announced a gradual effort to shift about 6 percent of DOD spending from lower priority measures to higher priority ones, with investment accounts to be a main beneficiary. If this effort succeeds, it could bolster procurement budgets enough to permit faster modernization. But much also depends upon whether DOD can reform its acquisition process to speed RDT&E programs and to buy new weapons at affordable costs. On this critical matter, the QDRP Report and QDR Report agree.

The outcome of their mutual efforts to reform the acquisition process is yet to be seen, and likely will be a function of how multiple RDT&E and procurement programs are handled by each Service component. Modernization of U.S. air forces seems best poised to operate at a steady rate that provides such new fighters as the F–35 JSF, F/A–18 A/B, and unmanned aerial systems. Modernization of ground forces is less certain. Cancellation of the Army's Future Combat Systems program for high-tech lightweight ground vehicles has led the Army to pursue a redesigned Ground Combat Vehicle program that is less technologically ambitious and less risky. If the Army opts for improvements to such existing vehicles as the Abrams tank, Bradley fighting vehicle, Stryker vehicle, and MRAP (Mine Resistant Ambush Protected) armored vehicle, new and better vehicles could be available for procurement in a few years in ways that would provide important marginal improvements, but not a great technological leap forward. But if the Army opts for an entirely new class of vehicles aimed at pushing the technology envelope further, it could face a more prolonged RDT&E effort and thus later procurement, perhaps near the end of this decade.

The Navy faces similar challenges in designing new warships in ways that balance near-term achievability with long-term technological progress. If by mid-decade or later the outcome is the modernizing of air forces but a slower modernization of ground and naval forces, this will produce a stronger U.S. military posture, but not in the faster, comprehensive ways favored by the QDRP Report and QDR Report. The key point, which applies to both reports, is that advocating reforms to the acquisition process makes sense, but actually implementing them is hard because of the many difficult RDT&E decisions that must be made one weapon at a time.

Is the QDRP Report too critical of the QDR Report in proposing that in the future, it should be scrapped? Although the QDR Report is far from perfect, a telling observation is that the QDRP could not have been written so well in the absence of an already published QDR Report to provide a benchmark and a model to criticize. Beyond this, the QDR Report may not be popular in some quarters outside DOD, but within DOD, it performs valuable analytical and planning functions that help inform many civilian and military personnel. Nothing comparable currently exists to take its place. Perhaps the QDRP is correct in judging that DOD could use its normal PPBES functions and documents to replace the QDR Report. But a noteworthy consideration is that the QDR Report was originally commissioned partly because the PPBES process was not producing a synthetic, comprehensive document to guide DOD strategy and planning. If the QDR

Report is abolished, DOD will need to conduct a formal internal strategy review every 4 years, as was done before the QDR Report was created, but these strategy reviews were always classified and unavailable across all of DOD, the U.S. Government, and the general public. If the QDR Report is scrapped, presumably this public communications task would have to be handled by restored Secretary of Defense annual posture statements, which earlier were as long and detailed as today's QDR Report. If the QDR Report is to be killed off, something similar will have to be created to replace it. Perhaps the solution is not to scrap future QDR Reports, but instead to prepare them more fully and carefully, with due attention not only to the near term, but the long term as well.

As for the QDRP Report's suggestion that an Independent Strategic Review Panel of experts be convened to produce strategic guidance before an incoming administration has had time to write its own national security strategy, this idea seemingly makes sense. In 2010, the North Atlantic Treaty Organization followed a similar recommendation by convening such a team of outside experts to provide guidance in the months before the Alliance set about the task of writing a new strategic concept. The result was a useful study (see chapter 6). Perhaps similarly useful studies could be written by Independent Strategic Review Panels in ways that give incoming administrations a useful infusion of outside advice. But ultimately, each new administration will need to go through the exercise of preparing its own national security strategy, its own QDR Report, and comparable studies by other departments and agencies. In this regard, the past and present are prologue.

CHAPTER FOUR

Nuclear Posture Review Report

To cope with new international dangers while making progress on President Barack Obama's call for ultimately achieving a world without nuclear weapons, the Nuclear Posture Review (NPR) Report—a 49-page document that focuses mainly on the next 5 to 10 years—identifies five key objectives for forging U.S. nuclear policies and making decisions about the future nuclear force posture:

- preventing nuclear proliferation and nuclear terrorism
- reducing the role of U.S. nuclear weapons in U.S. national security strategy
- maintaining strategic deterrence and stability at reduced nuclear force levels
- strengthening regional deterrence and reassuring U.S. allies and partners
- sustaining a safe, secure, and effective nuclear arsenal.

Pursuing these objectives, it states, will require a sustainable consensus that produces concerted efforts by a long succession of administrations and Congresses for many years to come.

Handling the Changing International Environment. The NPR Report judges that while the risk of global nuclear war has become remote owing to the end of the Cold War, the risk that nuclear weapons will actually be used has increased owing to other developments. Citing nuclear terrorism and nuclear proliferation as two principal dangers, it moves the task of preventing these scenarios and strengthening the global nonproliferation regime to the top of the U.S. nuclear security agenda. But it also calls for policies aimed at maintaining nuclear stability with Russia and China and countering threats posed by any nuclear-armed states in ways that protect the United States, as well as allies and partners, from nuclear threats or intimidation.

The NPR Report states that the most immediate and extreme threat today is nuclear terrorism (that is, al Qaeda or other terrorist groups gain access to nuclear weapons and use them against the United States and/or its allies). To date, it states, considerable progress has been made toward achieving a global "lockdown" of nuclear weapons, materials, and related technology, but much more work needs to be done; the United States and the international community currently have insufficient capabilities to detect, interdict, and defeat efforts to covertly deliver nuclear materials and weapons, as well as to minimize casualties and economic impact, and to attribute sources if a nuclear attack occurs.

Today's other pressing threat, the NPR Report argues, is nuclear proliferation. It particularly cites threats posed by North Korea and Iran, whose nuclear ambitions are violating nonproliferation obligations, increasing regional tensions, threatening to illicitly supply nuclear weapons and materials to other dangerous actors, and weakening the Nuclear Non-Proliferation Treaty (NPT). It further states that the potential for regional nuclear aggression by these states raises challenges to not only deterrence of them, but also the goal of reassuring allies and partners of their security. It holds that if allies and partners are not adequately assured of deterrence and their security, some will elect to acquire nuclear deterrent postures of their own in ways that could unravel the NPT regime and increase the likelihood of nuclear use. The NPR Report declares that the NPT remains a cornerstone of nonproliferation efforts and that its basic agreement—all parties have a right to peaceful nuclear power, states without nuclear weapons forsake them, and nuclear-armed states work toward disarmament—remains sound. But it also judges that because of ongoing noncompliance with the NPT, the nonproliferation regime, including the International Atomic Energy Agency (IAEA), urgently requires strengthening.

The NPR Report further judges that the U.S. nuclear interaction with Russia and potentially China poses muted but still existing dangers of its own in ways mandating careful management focused on maintaining strategic stability. Noting that both Russia and China are modernizing their nuclear postures, it cites the need to sign the New Strategic Arms Reduction Treaty (START) with Russia, which further reduces nuclear force levels on both sides, and to pursue a stabilizing dialogue with China. The combination of rising threats from nuclear terrorism and nuclear proliferation and still worrisome strategic interactions with Russia and China, it states, has altered the international nuclear security environment in basic ways that threaten to outpace the rate of U.S. adaptation and modification. Accordingly, it judges that in putting an end to Cold War thinking, the United States should:

- intensify efforts to build broad international support for the rigorous measures needed to prevent nuclear terrorism and nuclear proliferation

- pursue steps to enhance regional security architectures to reassure allies and partners that U.S. commitments to their defense remain strong and reliable

- continue striving for deeper nuclear reductions in negotiations with Russia

- lessen U.S. reliance on nuclear weapons in national security strategy in ways that respond to growing U.S. capabilities in conventional forces and missile defenses

- preserve a fully adequate nuclear force posture while making investments to ensure that the nuclear stockpile can be maintained without further nuclear testing.

This strategic agenda, the NRP Report states, has major implications for U.S. nuclear weapons policies and force structures. It observes that the massive nuclear arsenal inherited from the Cold War is poorly suited to addressing the challenges posed by suicidal terrorists and unfriendly states seeking nuclear weapons. It also calls for steps to better align nuclear policies and force structures with the most urgent priorities of preventing nuclear terrorism and nuclear proliferation. It acknowledges that for the foreseeable future, a strong U.S. nuclear force posture will be needed to safeguard deterrence, reassure allies and partners, and promote regional and global stability. But it also judges that because of fundamental changes in recent years—including the growth of unrivalled U.S. conventional military capabilities, major improvements in missile defenses, and easing of Cold War rivalries—the United States will be able to pursue its national security goals at significantly lower nuclear force levels and with reduced reliance upon nuclear weapons. In aspiring to build a new and deeper understanding of how U.S. weapons affect modern-era international dynamics, it reasons that:

- by reducing the role and number of nuclear weapons and thereby meeting its own NPT obligations, the United States can strengthen its ability to persuade NPT partners to pursue measures aimed at reinvigorating the nonproliferation regime and securing nuclear materials worldwide against theft or seizure by terrorist groups

- by maintaining a credible nuclear deterrent posture while reinforcing regional security architectures with missile defenses and other conventional military capabilities, the United States can reassure its nonnuclear allies and partners worldwide that their security is intact and that they do not need nuclear weapons

- by maintaining strategic stability with Russia and China while promoting transparency and mutual confidence, the United States can help create the conditions for moving toward a world without nuclear weapons, while building greater cooperation with them on addressing the threats of nuclear terrorism and nuclear proliferation

- by working to reduce the salience of nuclear weapons in international affairs, partly by further restricting the conditions under which U.S. nuclear weapons might be used, the United States can reverse the growing expectation that a world of many nuclear-armed powers lies ahead, decrease the incentives for additional countries to acquire nuclear weapons, reduce the likelihood of nuclear use, and promote the eventual elimination of nuclear weapons in a step-by-step manner

- by pursuing a sound stockpile management program for extending the life of existing U.S. nuclear weapons, while modernizing aging nuclear facilities and investing in human capital, the United States can substantially reduce the number of stockpiled nuclear weapons retained as a hedge against technological or geopolitical surprises and accelerate the dismantlement of unneeded nuclear weapons.

Preventing Nuclear Proliferation and Nuclear Terrorism. In elevating these two goals to the top of the U.S. nuclear security agenda, the NPR Report strongly affirms that the United States will lead efforts to strengthen the global nonproliferation regime and to accelerate efforts to prevent nuclear terrorism. To bolster the nonproliferation regime, it calls upon the United States to pursue measures aimed at:

- reversing the nuclear ambitions of North Korea and Iran by pursuing negotiations that offer integration into the international community if they comply, while further isolating and pressuring them if they do not

- strengthening IAEA safeguards by giving additional resources and authorities to the agency

- creating consequences for noncompliance, including by ensuring that states cannot escape such consequences by withdrawing from the NPT

- impeding sensitive nuclear trade by strengthening export controls and border controls, disrupting illicit proliferation networks, restricting transfer of dual-use enrichment and reprocessing technologies, making the Proliferation Security Initiative into a durable international institution, disrupting the financing of nuclear terrorism and proliferation networks, and developing a United Nations (UN) trust fund to assist countries in meeting their nonproliferation obligations

- promoting the peaceful uses of nuclear energy without increasing proliferation by pursuing the Global Nuclear Energy Partnership, international fuel banks, agreements by suppliers to take back spent fuel, creation of fuel repositories, and cradle-to-grave nuclear dual-use management.

To strengthen international efforts to prevent nuclear terrorism, the NPR Report calls upon the United States to:

- pursue the President's Prague Initiative, endorsed by UN Security Council Resolution 1887, to secure all vulnerable nuclear materials worldwide

- host summits aimed at fighting nuclear smuggling and terrorism, and at strengthening effective nuclear security measures

- increase funding by 25 percent for national nonproliferation programs

- accelerate the Global Threat Reduction Initiative by removing and securing vulnerable nuclear material, converting reactors to use fuels that cannot be used in nuclear weapons, and completing repatriation of U.S.-origin and Russian-origin highly enriched uranium from world research reactors

- accelerate the International Nuclear Material Protection and Cooperation Program to install nuclear security upgrades at Russian complexes and to expand cooperation with new countries beyond Russia and the former Soviet Union

- secure and eliminate weapons of mass destruction (WMD) and their means of delivery through threat reduction programs at Defense, State, and other departments, including the flagship Nunn-Lugar Cooperative Threat Reduction Program

- enhance national and international capabilities to detect and interdict smuggling of nuclear materials by expanding the Container Security Initiative to screen U.S.-bound cargo; pursue the Second Line of Defense Megaports Initiative to install radiation detectors at key borders, airports, and seaports; and build the 77-country Global Initiative to Combat Terrorism into a durable international institution

- continue to strengthen nuclear forensics efforts

- renew the U.S. commitment to hold fully accountable any state, terrorist group, or other nonstate actor that supports or enables terrorist efforts to obtain or use WMD.

In addition, the NPR Report states that the United States can help strengthen efforts to prevent nuclear terrorism and nuclear proliferation by ratifying New START and later pursing deeper nuclear reductions, ratifying the Comprehensive Test Ban Treaty, initiating negotiations on a Fissile Material Cut-off Treaty, working with Russia to eliminate 68 tons of unneeded weapons-grade plutonium, and beginning a comprehensive research, development, test, and evaluation (RDT&E) program that develops improved verification technologies and transparency measures.

Reducing the Role of U.S. Nuclear Weapons in National Security Strategy. The NPR Review proclaims that the fundamental role of nuclear weapons in deterring nuclear attack on the United States, its allies, and partners will remain unchanged. But it also announces that the time has arrived to further reduce the already declining role that nuclear weapons play in deterring and defending against conventional aggression and use of biological and chemical weapons (CBW). This step is possible, it claims, because old Cold War threats in Europe are gone and because U.S., allied, and partner militaries now provide a wide range of conventional options to deter and defeat conventional aggression by regional adversaries. Accordingly, it declares, the United States is now prepared to strengthen its longstanding assurance that it will not use or threaten to use nuclear weapons against nonnuclear states that are parties to the NPT and in compliance with nonproliferation obligations. This upgraded assurance, it states, is intended to underscore the security benefits of complying with the NPT and to persuade nonnuclear states to cooperate with efforts to strengthen the nonproliferation regime. In making this revised assurance, it continues, any nonnuclear state that uses CBW against the United States, its allies, or partners will be held accountable and will face a devastating conventional military response. It adds the caveat that the United States reserves the right to alter its assurance about not using nuclear weapons if warranted by the evolution and proliferation of biological weapons in ways that undermine U.S. capabilities to respond effectively with conventional forces.

In the case of countries that possess nuclear weapons and those not meeting their nonproliferation obligations, the NPR Report states, there remains a narrow range of contingencies in which U.S. nuclear weapons may still play a role in deterring a conventional or CBW attack against the United States, its allies, or partners. Therefore, the United States is not yet prepared to adopt a universal policy in which the sole purpose of nuclear weapons is to deter nuclear attack, but will instead work to establish the conditions under which such a policy could be safely adopted. Accordingly, the NPR Report adopts four principles for U.S. nuclear policies:

- The United States will meet its NPT commitments to pursue nuclear disarmament and will make demonstrable progress over the next 5 to 10 years.

- The United States will continue strengthening conventional capabilities and reduce the role of nuclear weapons in deterring nonnuclear attacks, with the goal of making the deterrence of nuclear attack the sole purpose of U.S. nuclear weapons.

- The United States would consider using nuclear weapons only in extreme circumstances to defend its vital interests and those of allies and partners.

- The United States will not use or threaten to use nuclear weapons against nonnuclear states that are in compliance with the NPT and their nonproliferation obligations.

Maintaining Strategic Deterrence and Stability at Reduced Nuclear Force Levels. The NPR Report begins this section by noting that although the United States and Russia have reduced their operationally deployed strategic nuclear force levels by 75 percent since the Cold War ended, both retain many more nuclear weapons than needed for deterrence. It portrays New START as an initial step toward further reducing force levels while preserving strategic stability. U.S. negotiating positions in the New START talks with Russia, it states, were derived from careful NPR analysis aimed at identifying emerging requirements for U.S. strategic nuclear weapons, the scope of potential reductions below the Moscow Treaty level of 2,200 deployed nuclear forces, and subsequent force limitations. After concluding that the United States should retain a nuclear triad, it states, the analysis determined the appropriate force structure for each leg of the triad: ballistic missile submarines (SSBNs) and submarine-launched ballistic missiles (SLBMs), intercontinental ballistic missiles (ICBMs), and nuclear-capable heavy bombers. The analysis focused on meeting four requirements:

- supporting strategic stability through an assured second-strike capability
- retaining sufficient forces in each leg to be able to hedge effectively by shifting emphasis from one triad leg to another in response to technological surprise or operational vulnerabilities
- retaining a margin above the minimum required nuclear force structure for the possible addition of nonnuclear prompt global strike capabilities, such as ICBMs and SLBMs, that would carry conventional weapons but still be accountable under New START
- maintaining the needed capabilities over the next several decades and more, including retaining a sufficient cadre of trained personnel and infrastructure.

Based on this analysis, the NPR Report declares that New START is based on the following mutual limits, which reduce force levels below the 2,200 nuclear warheads and 1,200 strategic delivery vehicles (SDVs) allowed by the expired Moscow Treaty. Accountable warheads are reduced by about 30 percent below the Moscow Treaty and SDVs are reduced by about 50 percent:

- a limit of 1,550 accountable strategic warheads
- a separate limit of 700 deployed SDVs: ICBMs, SLBMs, and heavy bombers
- a combined limit of 800 deployed and nondeployed ICBM launchers, SLBM launchers, and heavy bombers
- dual-capable bombers will count as one SDV and one warhead in recognition of the fact that heavy bombers do not pose a first-strike threat.

The NPR Report's conclusion that a triad posture should be retained under New START reflects the judgment that each leg of the triad offers unique advantages. SSBNs are highly survivable when deployed at sea, and SLBMs are not vulnerable to air defenses. Single-warhead ICBMs provide strong response capabilities and contribute to stability. Heavy bombers can be deployed forward in a crisis to signal deterrence and reassure allies and partners. Three legs provide a hedge against the risk that one might suffer a major technical or operational failure. A three-leg posture, with each leg capable of withstanding a surprise attack, is far harder to destroy than a single-leg posture. Each leg of the posture offers important targeting capabilities: ballistic missiles can respond rapidly with great accuracy and bombers can strike a wide variety of targets ranging from cities to military installations. Beyond this, as the NPR Report states, a three-leg posture provides options for uploading additional nuclear warheads as a technical hedge against any future problems with delivery systems or warheads or a fundamental deterioration in the security environment.

In providing guidance on the future of the triad under New START, the NPR Report addresses all three legs individually. The United States, it states, will retain all 14 *Ohio*-class SSBNs for the near term while considering a reduction to 12 SSBNs late in the decade. The development of a new SSBN to eventually replace the aging *Ohio*-class SSBNs will commence. The United States will retain 450 Minuteman III ICBMs, de-MIRV (multiple independently targetable reentry vehicle) them by equipping them with only one warhead, extend the service life of the Minuteman IIIs, and initiate study of a follow-on ICBM. The United States will retain a heavy bomber force of 76 B–52H bombers and 18 B–2 bombers that can be equipped with nuclear weapons but are "dual-use" because they are not placed on nuclear alert and can carry conventional bombs and missiles. The B–2 bombers will be upgraded in the coming years.

In addition, the NPR Report provides steps aimed at maximizing presidential decision time in a nuclear crisis:

- maintain the current alert posture of U.S. nuclear forces, with heavy bombers off full-time alert, nearly all ICBMs on alert, and a significant number of SSBNs deployed at sea

- continue the practice of "open-ocean" targeting so that if a missile is inadvertently launched, it will land in the open ocean

- make investments in the U.S. command and control system to enhance its resiliency and capabilities for fully deliberate control of the force in a crisis

- explore new forms of ICBM basing that could enhance survivability.

The NPR Report also provides guidance on future nonstrategic (tactical) nuclear weapons. It notes that these weapons have been reduced dramatically since the Cold War ended. Today, it states, the United States keeps only a limited number of these weapons deployed in Europe, plus a small number stored domestically, that can be promptly deployed in a crisis. All such weapons have been withdrawn from Asia. It argues that particularly because Russia retains large numbers of nonstrategic nuclear weapons, they should be included in any future reduction agreements with Russia beyond New START, but in close consultation with North Atlantic Treaty Organization (NATO) Allies. The NPR Report states that, in cooperation with allies and partners, the United States has determined the Air Force will retain a dual-capable fighter as new F–35s arrive and extend the life span of the B–61 nuclear bomb, and the Navy will retire the nuclear-tipped cruise missile (Tactical Land Attack Missile–Nuclear).

Looking toward the future of nuclear arms control negotiations with Russia, the NPR Report judges that further significant bilateral reductions below New START levels should be pursued. Any such reductions, it cautions, must continue to strengthen the deterrence of adversaries, strategic stability vis-à-vis Russia and China, and reassurance of allies and partners. The United States, it states, is committed to further reducing its own nuclear arsenal, but because large disparities with Russian nuclear forces would not be conducive to a stable long-term relationship, Russia should join the United States in this enterprise.

Strengthening Regional Deterrence and Reassuring U.S. Allies and Partners. In this section, the NPR Report points out that U.S. allies and partners are on the front line of a changing global security environment. Some of them enjoy unprecedented security and are therefore seeking reduced reliance on nuclear weapons, but others—neighbored by major nuclear-armed powers seeking stronger regional roles, potential aggressors, nuclear proliferators, potential WMD smugglers, and failing states—have been led to seek enhanced security ties to the United States. This complex milieu dictates that the United States must continue to reaffirm its commitment to the security of its allies and partners through not only words, but also deeds. Credibly underwriting these commitments, it continues, includes maintaining firm political ties with them, strengthening U.S. and allied conventional capabilities, and continuing to provide extended deterrence.

Such commitments, the NPR Report states, will retain a nuclear dimension for as long as nuclear threats to allies and partners remain. Today, it judges, a credible U.S. nuclear umbrella is provided by a combination of means: U.S. strategic forces, nonstrategic weapons that are forward deployed, and U.S.-based nuclear weapons that can be deployed forward quickly in response to regional contingencies. In Europe, it states, the continuing presence of a small number of nuclear weapons contributes to NATO cohesion and reassures member nations who feel exposed to regional threats. As a result, decisions to alter the Alliance's nuclear posture should be taken carefully and only after thorough review. In Asia, it reports, the withdrawal of U.S. forward-deployed nuclear weapons means that extended deterrence is mainly carried out by bilateral security agreements with several nations, U.S. conventional forces, central strategic forces, and the capacity to redeploy nonstrategic nuclear forces if necessary. The United States, it states, is pursuing strategic dialogues with its allies and partners in East Asia and the Middle East to determine how best to reassure them that U.S. extended deterrence efforts remain credible and effective.

Enhancing regional security architectures, the NPR Report argues, is a key part of U.S. strategy for strengthening deterrence while reducing the role and numbers of nuclear weapons. These regional architectures, it states, are to include effective missile defenses, counter-WMD capabilities, conventional power-projection capabilities, and integrated command and control, all underwritten by strong political commitments. Although the U.S. nuclear posture has a vital role to play in these regional architectures, strengthening their nonnuclear elements is vital. Effective missile defenses are essential, and credible deterrence requires land, naval, and air forces capable of fighting limited and large-scale conflicts in antiaccess environments.

Accordingly, the NPR Report calls for the following initiatives:

- continue to work with allies and partners to build enhanced regional security architectures, including nonnuclear capabilities for deterrence, improved partner capacities, and combined exercises and training
- continue and expand ongoing bilateral and multilateral discussions with allies and partners to determine the most effective ways to enhance regional stability in Europe, Northeast and Southwest Asia, and the Middle East
- work with allies and partners to respond to regional threats by deploying effective missile defenses in multiple regions through a phased adaptive approach
- deepen consultations with allies and partners on policies and combined postures to prevent proliferation and to credibly deter aggression
- strengthen counter-WMD capabilities for defeating chemical or biological attacks
- develop improved nonnuclear prompt global strike capabilities for defeating time-urgent regional threats
- develop and deploy more effective capabilities for real-time intelligence, surveillance, and reconnaissance operations
- retain the capability to forward deploy U.S. nuclear weapons on fighters and heavy bombers.

Maintaining a Safe, Secure, and Effective Nuclear Arsenal. The NPR Report declares that the United States is committed to ensure that its stockpile of nuclear weapons remains safe, effective, and secure. It announces decisions on how best to meet this long-term obligation. Today's nuclear weapons, it notes, have aged well beyond their originally planned life spans, and many excess nuclear weapons are awaiting dismantlement. Since 1992, the United States has not developed, procured, and tested new nuclear weapons to replace aging weapons. Instead, it has stopped nuclear testing and relied upon a Stockpile Stewardship Program to ensure the safety and reliability of existing weapons while extending their lives by refurbishing them to nearly original specifications. Calling for a continuation of this practice, the NPR Report reaches the following conclusions regarding future stockpile management decisions:

- The United States will not conduct nuclear testing, and will pursue ratification and entry into force of the Comprehensive Test Ban Treaty.

- The United States will not develop new nuclear weapons. Life Extension Programs (LEPs) for existing weapons will use only nuclear components based on previously tested designs, and will not support new missions or capabilities.

- The United States will study options for ensuring the safety, security, and reliability of nuclear warheads on a case-by-case basis consistent with the congressionally mandated Stockpile Management Program, and will consider the full range of LEP approaches: refurbishment of existing warheads, reuse of nuclear components from different warheads, and replacement of nuclear components.

- In engineering development for warhead LEPs, the United States will give strong preference to refurbishment or reuse. Replacement of nuclear components will be undertaken only if absolutely necessary.

- The United States will retain the smallest possible stockpile consistent with military and strategic needs.

- Using this approach, the NPR Report urges full funding of ongoing LEPs for the W–76 submarine-based warhead, completion of the LEP study and subsequent activities for the B–61 bomb, and initiation of an LEP study for the W–78 ICBM warhead.

In addition, the NPR Report calls for stronger efforts to improve the eroding complex of laboratories and supporting facilities that handle nuclear weapons, recruit a skilled workforce, and strengthen science, technology, and engineering assets for addressing future warhead policies and programs.

Is a World Without Nuclear Weapons Achievable? In addressing this question, the NPR Report acknowledges that nuclear weapons continue to play a major contributing role in U.S. national security strategy and its quest for stable international security affairs. It also acknowledges the importance of efforts to strengthen U.S. nuclear forces even as negotiations seek deeper reductions than envisioned by New START. Creating a world without nuclear weapons, it judges, will be a long-term and demanding proposition that will require not only ambitious arms control negotiations but also the settlement of regional disputes and the halting of nuclear proliferation. But unless the effort is launched and pursued seriously, the NPR Report concludes, it will never succeed or even make significant headway, and if abject failure is the result, the nuclear world of tomorrow could be significantly more dangerous.

Strengths, Shortfalls, and Lingering Issues. Compared to earlier U.S. Government unclassified studies on nuclear issues, the NPR Report is longer, more complete, and more informative. The report's most ambitious goal is fostering a world without nuclear weapons—a vision that has been praised by some observers, but dismissed as naïve and unachievable by others. Notwithstanding its admission that this goal is a long-term prospect for the far-distant future, the NPR Report is mostly preoccupied with practicalities of handling emerging challenges in the near- and mid-term, and here its approach is decidedly pragmatic. To handle these challenges, it puts forth a large set of policies and initiatives intended to achieve U.S. national security objectives. The key issue is whether these actions are well conceived and sufficiently comprehensive, and whether they will succeed in ways that accomplish their purposes.

A main strength of the NPR Report is its elevation of countering nuclear proliferation and nuclear terrorism to the top of the U.S. nuclear security agenda. Nobody would question that handling these dangerous challenges is compellingly important, and that the QDR Report makes a concerted effort to chart the path ahead. But while many of its ideas are widely supported, others are controversial. Its agenda for preventing nuclear proliferation reflects a mixture of both. In a bold departure, the NPR Report advances the proposition that nuclear restraint by the United States—for example, such actions as reducing its own nuclear posture and further restricting the conditions under which it would use nuclear weapons in war—will help motivate countries to embrace the NPT and the global nonproliferation regime. Restraint will also prompt others to refrain from acquiring or using nuclear weapons themselves. Is this proposition a reliable guide to effective U.S. policies? Perhaps so but, to a degree, it seems to suggest that past U.S. policies for deploying nuclear forces and using them to enhance deterrence have played a role in accelerating WMD proliferation rather than retarding it. The historical record on this offers a rather mixed appraisal.

Most likely, the powerful U.S. nuclear arsenal helped stimulate the Soviet nuclear buildup early during the Cold War, but had the United States forsaken its own nuclear buildup, it likely would have found itself unable to contain and deter a nuclear-equipped Soviet Union. In recent years, U.S. nuclear weapons may have played a contributing role in motivating North Korea and Iran to pursue their own nuclear weapons. However, these two countries are dangerous adversaries that may have sought these weapons irrespective of whether the United States was reducing its nuclear posture at a faster rate than has been pursued over the past two decades. Beyond this, U.S. nuclear guarantees have undeniably played a strong contributing role in persuading allies and partners—for instance, Germany and Japan— not to acquire their own nuclear weapons. Also, the U.S. nuclear arsenal seemingly played no role in motivating India and Pakistan to acquire nuclear weapons; the two countries were acting for reasons that reflected their own rivalry in South Asia as well as China's nuclear posture, not the U.S. nuclear posture or the global nuclear balance.

The key point of this historical record is that nuclear proliferation responds to underlying geopolitical imperatives and a complex action-reaction cycle in which the U.S. nuclear arsenal is not always a potent influence on other countries and sometimes retards nuclear proliferation rather than stimulates it. Precisely for this reason, the NPR Report makes clear that U.S. nuclear commitments to allies and friends will remain strong, as will deterrent warnings to nuclear-equipped adversaries, even as the United States strives to scale back the role of nuclear weapons in its global security strategy and reduces its nuclear posture. If nuclear proliferation accelerates in dangerous ways in future years, it likely will compel the United States to extend its nuclear umbrella over a larger number of states than today, including in the Middle East. In this setting, the NPR Report is undoubtedly correct in judging that the United States can help set an example that encourages membership in the nonproliferation regime by showing self-restraint in its own nuclear activities. Whether this approach can be an across-the-board coda for future U.S. nuclear strategy, force posture, and deterrence commitments is another matter entirely. When the dust settles some years from now, U.S. nuclear weapons may play a role that is as large, or even larger, than they play today.

U.S. self-restraint aside, the NPR Report puts forth a set of wide-ranging political and diplomatic steps aimed at halting nuclear proliferation, including a stronger IAEA, impediments to sensitive nuclear trade, peaceful uses of nuclear energy, and consequences for noncompliance. All of these steps make strategic sense. At the top of this list is a U.S. policy to reverse the nuclear ambitions of North Korea and Iran by engaging them politically with offers of favorable treatment if they comply, and threats of further isolation and pressure if they do not. Thus far, this well-oiled approach has not prevented North Korea from openly developing nuclear weapons, and it does not seem to be derailing Iran from its nuclear path. What will happen if, a year or more from now, Iran emerges with nuclear weapons and long-range missiles for delivering them? Will diplomatic engagement and political pressure still be appropriate, or will the United States need to apply nuclear deterrence to Iran, or even launch military strikes against its nuclear weapons, missiles, and facilities? The NPR Report is silent on these sensitive questions, but clear answers may soon be needed.

The NPR Report also puts forth a large set of measures and programs to prevent nuclear terrorism, including enhanced homeland defense programs and accelerated international cooperation in this domain. These steps all make sense. But will they be adequate to get the job done by both denying terrorists access to nuclear weapons and preventing their use if acquired? Only in-depth technical analysis can answer this question, but the NPR Report does not provide such analysis. At the end of its list of measures and programs, the NPR Report renews the U.S. commitment to hold "fully accountable" any state, terrorist group, or other nonstate actor that supports or enables terrorist efforts to obtain or use nuclear weapons or other WMD. But what does *fully accountable* mean, and how can it be applied not only to states that can be attacked but also to terrorist groups and other nonstate actors that are often hard to attack and, under some circumstances, even hard to identify? The NPR Report is silent on retaliatory mechanisms, but if deterrence is to work in this arena, in-depth analysis of such mechanisms and associated strategies will clearly be needed—perhaps sooner rather than later.

One of the NPR Report's most high-profile measures is its strengthening of already existing assurances that U.S. nuclear weapons will not be used against nonnuclear states that are meeting their nonproliferation obligations. As intended, this step likely will play a role in enhancing the attractiveness of membership in the NPT club. But it is not new when judged in historical terms. In the last 50 years, the United States has fought multiple conventional wars against adversaries that were not nuclear armed, and it has never seriously intended to use nuclear weapons against them. In the future, the NPR Report implies, the United States will never use nuclear weapons against nonnuclear powers even if they are attacking close American allies with conventional weapons and are threatening to conquer them. If this is new U.S. strategy, it may come as a disturbing surprise to several close allies—for instance, those in NATO and South Korea—that have faced serious conventional threats and always have taken comfort in the idea that if combined U.S.-allied conventional defenses buckle, U.S. nuclear weapons will come to the rescue. After all, NATO military strategy during the Cold War called for nuclear weapons to help offset the Alliance's vulnerable conventional defenses, and, in recent years, NATO has not cast aside this provision or embraced a "no first use" doctrine. Nor have key allies in Asia done so.

Troubling questions arise about the theory and precepts of the new nuclear non-use pledge. Why does the lack of nuclear weapons make a conventional aggressor entirely immune from U.S. nuclear reprisals? Why is U.S. military strategy determined not by the safety and security of vulnerable allies that belong to U.S-led alliances, but instead by the presence or absence of nuclear armaments in the hands of aggressors? Is U.S. strategy now stating that if vital American interests are threatened by an adversary with imposing conventional forces but no nuclear weapons, the United States will keep its nuclear weapons holstered even if they are the only recourse for protecting those interests? If such a nonnuclear adversary can conduct conventional aggression without fearing U.S. nuclear reprisals, why would a nuclear-armed power hesitate to commit similar aggression if it promises to keep its own nuclear forces out of the contest? If the United States is unwilling to pursue nuclear escalation against enemies that lack nuclear weapons, why should allies and partners trust that it is willing to escalate in the more dangerous presence of enemies with nuclear weapons? In trying to answer these questions, the NPR Report states that if nuclear weapons are to be safely forsaken, future U.S. and allied conventional postures will need to be made strong enough to perform their defense missions. Doubtless so, but sometimes achieving this goal is easier said than done. Although stalwart conventional defenses can be erected, normally they cannot be made impregnable. There will almost always be a degree of risk that nuclear forces were, in the past, designed to lessen, even after they already had been relegated to the backwaters of common defense strategy. To claim that nuclear weapons are a last resort is one thing, but to assert that they are no longer any resort at all is something else, even if the caveat is that this formula applies only to nonnuclear adversaries.

The NPR Report tries to work its way out of its strategy conundrum in this area by stating that U.S. nuclear weapons could still be used to counter conventional aggression or CBW use by nuclear-armed states. In doing so, it seems to presume that if future adversaries possess menacing conventional forces, they likely will come equipped with nuclear weapons. Furthermore, it states that owing to superior U.S. and allied conventional means, such contingencies are narrow in range yet plausible. As a result, it declares, the United States is not yet prepared to adopt a universal policy that the sole purpose of nuclear weapons is to deter nuclear attack. Clearly this is a wise decision. But is the NPR Report correct in judging that plausible contingencies involving successful conventional aggression by a nuclear-armed adversary are truly small in number? What if Russia attacks the vulnerable Baltic states, or North Korea attacks South Korea, or China attacks Taiwan, or a nuclear-armed Iran attacks the Gulf Cooperation Council states of the Persian Gulf and tries to close the Strait of Hormuz? If plausible contingencies can be easily imagined in all major regions, this suggests that the era of nuclear-backed conventional aggression is far from being over, is still flourishing, and may be growing. If so, U.S. strategy for blending conventional defense with nuclear deterrence has more to consider than the NPR Report implies.

The NPR Report's advocacy of New START is controversial in some quarters because this treaty allegedly may be manipulated to constrain the United States from such measures as deploying mobile ICBMs and missile defenses, and may leave the Russians too much wiggle room for modernizing their nuclear forces. After a vigorous debate, the Senate ratified New START by 71 to 26 in December 2010. Regardless of how New START criticisms are appraised, the underlying issue is whether the proposed future U.S. nuclear posture—a still existing triad with 700 deployable SDVs and 1,550 warheads—will be adequate to meet enduring U.S. nuclear requirements for deterrence and warfighting. Confident adequacy seems the appropriate judgment, but questions begin arising when ever deeper force cuts are contemplated. On the surface, only a few SDVs and warheads appear capable of inflicting all the nuclear damage that could be wanted. But over past years, many studies have shown that when the demands of deterrence, survivable retaliation, and wartime targeting are added up, nuclear force requirements multiply rapidly and soon reach unanticipated levels. Beyond this, the new global nuclear setting involves more than the U.S.-Russia bilateral relationship; it now includes China, North Korea, potentially Iran, and possibly other countries that might have to be factored into the future U.S. force-sizing equation. A sensible conclusion is that if the U.S. Government is to pursue nuclear force cuts far deeper than New START, it is best advised to have its analytical house in order. Among other things, studies should examine the detailed mathematics of how U.S. and Russian nuclear forces should be reduced safely in a global setting of multiple nuclear-armed powers, so that the consequence is existing deterrence and stability, not the opposite.

The NPR Report makes an important contribution by calling for creation of new regional security architectures in such key regions as Europe, Asia, and the Middle East. As it implies, each region must be treated on a case-by-case basis. In this arena, the NPR Report is strong in its assessment of military requirements; it implies that such architectures can be built on a combination of improved conventional forces and missile defenses that lessen the traditional roles of nuclear weapons. Perhaps this treatment is correct, but in its preoccupation with military preparations, it neglects to discuss in any depth the underlying political foundations for such regional architectures. Years of U.S. experience going back to the Cold War and afterward have shown that the task of building solid political foundations is complex and hard, but must be undertaken well before the military superstructure is added. Perhaps Europe and Asia already possess much of this political foundation as well as the necessary military superstructure, but if Iran acquires nuclear weapons, the same cannot be said of the Middle East and Persian Gulf, where discussions with allies and partners are in early stages. If the United States, its allies, and partners must erect new security architecture there with the deterrence of Iran foremost in mind, they will have their work cut out—even if the NPR Report is not explicit on this point.

Finally, the NPR Report puts forth a coherent agenda for maintaining a safe, secure, and effective nuclear stockpile by not testing nuclear weapons, upgrading existing warheads and components, retiring unneeded warheads, and improving the facility infrastructure with better complexes and competent people. It prescribes a way to support the force posture with fewer warheads, avoid the contentious path of developing new warheads, and lower budget costs. But this agenda is neither inexpensive nor devoid of controversies. Its rejection of new weapons in favor of upgrading old weapons is controversial among some critics, who believe that new weapons are needed. Its proposals for facility infrastructure improvements are criticized by some observers who judge that the necessary funds and activities will not be forthcoming. Such criticisms aside, the NPR Report's basic policies make sense on issues of great technical complexity, but debates over specific warheads, development designs, and investment plans are likely to linger.

Ballistic Missile Defense Review Report

The Ballistic Missile Defense Review (BMDR) Report is a 48-page document that establishes new strategic and military directions for the coming phases of U.S. missile defense efforts over the next decade and beyond. Not intended to defend against the large Russian intercontinental ballistic missile (ICBM) force, the missile defense is principally focused on providing protection against nuclear attacks launched by North Korea, Iran, and other regional adversaries. It does so mainly by scaling back, but not eliminating, the Ground-based Midcourse Defense (GMD) system inherited from the Bush administration, canceling the so-called GMD Site Three in Poland, and accelerating plans to deploy increasingly sophisticated Standard Missle–3 (SM–3) interceptors, sensors, and command, control, communications, and intelligence (C³I) systems. Whereas the GMD system was focused primarily on providing homeland defense of the United States, the SM–3 program is mainly intended to provide missile defense protection of key regions, including Europe, Asia, and the Middle East. As Secretary Robert Gates states in his memorandum introducing the BMDR Report, defense against near-term regional threats is now a top priority of U.S. missile defense plans, programs, and capabilities.

The historical context is important to understanding the BMDR Report's contents. At the height of the Cold War during the 1960s, the Department of Defense (DOD) was pursuing vigorous research, development, test, and evaluation (RDT&E) programs for shooting down Soviet ICBMs and warheads with interceptor missiles. Careful study of the offense-defense interaction, however, showed that the United States could not be protected against massive damage in a nuclear war, that an ineffective and costly missile defense system could not be risked, and that such a system would accelerate the nuclear arms race. The result of subsequent U.S.-Soviet negotiations was an arms control treaty of the 1970s that ruled out large missile defenses on both sides, in the hope of fostering greater stability in the arms race. As a result, the United States was left wholly unprotected against missile attack.

When the Reagan administration took power in 1981, it questioned the wisdom of having no missile defenses and therefore launched a major RDT&E effort—called the Strategic Defense Initiative—to investigate the prospects for employing new technologies and systems that could work effectively. Despite large expenditures in multiple areas, no missile defenses were deployed during the 1980s and 1990s. But RDT&E efforts began focusing on the idea of creating a small missile defense posture that could protect the United States against limited ICBM threats posed by such regional adversaries as North Korea. Maturation of this idea and its technologies led the Bush administration in 2002 to authorize deployment of the GMD system, which was composed of 44 missiles at two sites in the United States (Alaska and California), and 10 missiles at the third site in Poland. Focused mainly on protecting the U.S. homeland, the GMD system did not provide significant missile defenses for protecting overseas-deployed U.S. military forces or key regional allies against threats to them.

The BMDR Report argues that missile threats from such adversaries as North Korea and Iran are growing in quantity and quality. Over the coming decade, it states, such adversaries can be expected to develop short-range ballistic missiles (SRBMs), medium-range ballistic missiles (MRBMs), and intermediate-range ballistic missiles (IRBMs) that can strike targets in nearby regions, and perhaps ICBMs capable of striking the United States. For both countries, such missiles are already being tested, and their future deployment in menacing numbers seems likely. In addition, North Korea already has nuclear weapons, while Iran may be developing them. The worrisome risk is that for North Korea and Iran, and perhaps for others over the long haul, nuclear weapons could be mounted atop long-range ballistic missiles, thereby rendering them capable of inflicting immense damage on neighboring states and even the United States. Beyond this, the BMDR Report argues, nuclear-tipped missiles could enable North Korea, Iran, and others to pursue peacetime coercion of neighbors that include many allies and partners of the United States. Defending against these threats, it judges, is imperative.

Credible hope, the BMDR Report asserts, comes from the rapid progress that U.S. RDT&E programs for missile defense have been making recently in the form of better interceptors, radars and sensors, and C^3I systems. The principal challenge, it states, is to take advantage of this progress by forging a revised missile defense strategy anchored in new programs. Together these provide deterrence of attack on the U.S. homeland, extended deterrence of attacks on allies and partners, and reassurance of those allies and partners. In this new strategy, deterrence is achieved not mainly by threatening nuclear retaliation, but by possessing interceptors capable of shooting down enemy nuclear missiles during the midcourse phase of their trajectory, thereby denying the adversary confidence that a nuclear attack, or the threat of such an attack, could achieve its strategic goals.

Accordingly, the BMDR Report puts forth six policy priorities for guiding ballistic missile defense efforts:

- The United States will continue to defend the homeland from limited ballistic missile attack.

- The United States will defend deployed U.S. forces from regional missile threats while also protecting allies and partners and enabling them to defend themselves.

- New missile defense capabilities must undergo realistic operational testing that demonstrates their effectiveness before they are deployed—a "fly before buy" approach will be followed.

- The commitment to new BMD capabilities must be fiscally sustainable over the long term—affordability will be important in the strategic calculus.

- U.S. BMD capabilities must be adaptable and flexible to adjust to changing future threats.

- The United States will seek to lead expanded international efforts for missile defense.

Defending the Homeland. The BMDR Report judges that currently the United States is adequately defended against limited ICBM attacks by the already deployed GMD posture of 30 Ground-based Interceptors (GBI, 26 in Alaska and 4 in California), early warning radars at four sites at home and abroad (Greenland and the United Kingdom), afloat radar systems, and a sophisticated command and control infrastructure. Accordingly, it states, DOD will scale back the original continental United States missile deployment plan from 44 GBI to the 30 GBI already deployed, and cancel or restructure some RDT&E programs (for example, the Airborne Laser Program) that have not succeeded. To preserve an adequate capability for the future and hedge against uncertainty, it states, DOD will pursue a vigorous RDT&E effort in GMD system enhancements that include more GBI testing, the SM–3 Block IIB missile, new missiles for intercepting long-range missiles early in flight, improved capacity to defeat countermeasures and achieve kinetic kills, and improved sensor networks that include airborne and space-based sensors. In addition, it states, DOD will complete construction of the final 14 GBI silos, which will provide a reserve capacity to rapidly deploy 8 more GBI missiles from the test pool.

Defending Against Regional Threats. In pursuing regional defense, the BMDR Report states, the United States has made considerable progress at developing and fielding essential capabilities for protecting against SRBMs and MRBMs. These assets, it continues, include increasingly capable Patriot batteries for point defense against SRBMs, the powerful AN/TPY–2 X-band radar for detecting and tracking ballistic missiles, soon-to-be-deployed Terminal High Altitude Area Defense (THAAD) batteries for intercepting SRBMs and MRBMs, and the sea-based SM–3 Block 1A interceptor aboard Aegis-equipped ships. Judging, however, that current capabilities are modest against emerging missile threats, it provides added funds for procuring more THAAD and SM–3 Block 1A interceptors, upgrading more Navy ships to incorporate Aegis BMD capabilities, and acquiring more AN/TPY radars. In addition, it puts forth an expanded program for the near term by developing a land-based SM–3 system, called "Aegis Ashore," that can be moved from one site to another. Aegis Ashore is to be ready by 2015. The report notes that DOD expects to have available a more capable SM–3 interceptor, the Block 1B, by 2015. The Block 1B, it states, will have an improved seeker capability for better target discrimination and greater area coverage. Additional near-term measures will include the continued development of an improved C^3I and battle-management system, improved sensors and situational awareness, an airborne infrared sensor, and an exploratory effort to develop improved early intercept capabilities by shortening the time needed to identify and track incoming missiles.

Turning to long-term measures, the BMDR Report states that toward the end of the decade, the new SM–3 Block IIA will have a higher burnout velocity and a more advanced seeker that will make it much more capable than the SM–3 Block IA and IB and provide greater regional coverage. It further reports that a SM–3 Block IIB missile is in the initial phase of technology assessment and development. This missile, it states, will provide added improvements in burnout velocity, divert capability, and regional coverage, and will provide some early intercept capability against long-range missiles. Investments, it states, are also being made to develop a better capacity to uplink data from multiple sensors as well as persistent overhead sensors in space that could detect and track launching of multiple missiles in ways that would reduce the need for terrestrial sensors and the size of deployed missile defenses. Funding this Precision Tracking and Space System, it states, is an important priority for the current DOD budget and Future Years Defense Plan.

Pursuing Integrated Regional Postures. Arguing that while past approaches to building regional missile defenses have proceeded from the bottom up, the BMDR Report asserts that future policies must be based on "top-down" thinking in strategic terms. It states that planning must begin with overarching, integrated core concepts that take U.S. and allied roles into account and then address the details of programs to create the appropriate set of missile intercep-tors, C^3 systems, sensors, and other assets. Accordingly, the BMDR Report puts forth three principles to guide development of regional approaches to achieve deterrence and pursue such other security goals as enhanced alliance cohesion, effective use of scarce resources, and focus on real threats and proven solutions. These goals are:

- Regional missile defense must be built on a strong foundation of improved security, cooperative relationships, and appropriate burden-sharing between the United States and its allies and partners in ways that, along with enhanced conventional capabilities, reduce reliance upon nuclear weapons for deterrence.

- The United States will pursue a phased adaptive approach (PAA) tailored to the individual requirements and opportunities of each region in ways that do not require a global structure that integrates all allies into a uniform architecture.

- The United States will develop flexible and mobile missile defenses that can be relocated among theaters and scaled upward or downward because the demand for missile defenses within each region over the next decade will exceed supply.

The BMDR Report focuses especially on the agenda of applying the PAA to Europe. It states that the earlier plan to deploy a GMD defense site in Poland along with radars in the Czech Republic was cancelled not because it failed to make sense some years ago, but because the emerging SM–3 missile and associated assets provide a more effective approach to defense against missile threats from the south. For Europe, the BMDR Report puts forth a four-phase plan:

- In Phase 1 (2011 timeframe), existing missile defenses will be deployed to defend against SRBM and MRBM threats. By using Aegis ships, SM–3 Block IA interceptors, radars, and associated assets, the result-ing missile posture will aspire to protect vulnerable portions of south-ern Europe.

- In Phase 2 (2015 timeframe), missile defenses will be enhanced by deploying SM–3 Block IB missiles, additional sensors, better C³ systems, and a land-based SM–3 site to expand coverage to additional North Atlantic Treaty Organization (NATO) Allies.

- In Phase 3 (2018 timeframe), coverage against MRBMs and IRBMs will be improved with a second land-based SM–3 site located in northern Europe as well as deployment of the SM–3 Block IIA missile, thereby extending coverage to all NATO Allies in Europe.

- In Phase 4 (2020 timeframe), additional capability will come from deployment of the SM–3 Block II B, which will provide protection against ICBMs launched from the Middle East against the United States and Europe.

The BMDR Report's discussion of future U.S. PAAs for Asia and the Middle East is less concrete. It notes that although the United States works through the NATO multilateral defense structure in Europe, it relies on bilateral alliances with key states in Asia and less formal relationships with a number of allies and partners in the Middle East. These dissimilar situations, it states, produce differing patterns of cooperation with the United States on ballistic missile defense, and have implications for the authorities under which the United States is able to operationally employ defenses to protect local allies and partners. In Asia, the BMDR Report states, the United States and Japan already cooperate in interoperable ways and are working together to develop a future missile defense system. In the Middle East, the United States and Israel are involved in production of the Arrow 2 missile and other RDT&E activities, and the United States is beginning to work with some Gulf Cooperation Council partners. Its main conclusion is that because the foundations for applying the PAA in these three regions are different, the pathways forward for U.S. missile defense deployments will be different, too—but it is vague on the exact pathways for Asia and the Middle East.

Strengthening International Cooperation. The BMDR Report asserts that the goal of expanding international efforts and cooperation on missile defense is being pursued on a dual track: developing and fielding robust, pragmatic, and cost-effective capabilities; and engaging in international cooperation on a broad range of missile defense–related activities, such as technological and industrial cooperation with multiple countries including Russia. As part of this effort, the BMDR Report states, the United States is engaged in an interagency review of its export control system in order to provide improved ways to facilitate allied missile defense efforts while denying transfer of technology to adversaries.

In Europe, the BMDR Report states, the United States is committed to implementing the PAA within a NATO context. In late 2009, NATO foreign ministers welcomed the U.S. PAA and declared that it reinforces the Alliance's central role in missile defense in Europe. In practical terms, this means that the European PAA will be the U.S. national contribution to a NATO missile defense capability. Accordingly, the BMDR Report states, the United States supports a potential NATO decision to adopt the role of missile defense of allied territory and population. Likewise, it continues, the United States supports NATO's ongoing effort to build and strengthen its program for an integrated command and control system for missile defense, which is called Active Layered Theater Missile Defense (ALTMD). The BMDR Report declares that while the ALTMD is currently designed to link together Allied assets for protecting deployed forces, it could be expanded to coordinate missile defense efforts to protect Allied populations and territory. In this context, it states, Poland and the Czech Republic will play a role in the PAA, and the United States is working with multiple Allies to develop and deploy missile defenses such as naval vessels with Aegis capabilities that could be linked together to create a networked NATO defense system. A primary U.S. emphasis, it claims, is to produce effective Alliance missile defenses and appropriate burden-sharing.

In East Asia, the BMDR Report states, the United States has a range of cooperative relationships, with Japan being a principal BMD partner. Japan, it judges, has acquired a layered integrated missile defense system that includes Aegis ships with SM–3 missiles, Patriot PAC–3 missiles, early warning radars, and a command and control system. The United States and Japan are pursuing regular training for cooperative missile defense, and are co-developing the SM–3 Block IIA interceptor. It lists South Korea as another important BMD partner that has indicated an interest in acquiring a missile defense capability that includes land-based and sea-based systems, as well as early warning radars and a command and control system. Bilateral discussions, it states, are also taking place with Australia and other countries in the region. In the Middle East, the BMDR Report portrays Israel as a leading BMD partner through common RDT&E programs such as the Arrow missile, plus training and exercises aimed at promoting operational cooperation. In the Persian Gulf, it states, the United States has a continuous missile defense presence and is seeking to build upon a Bilateral Air Defense Initiative to strengthen cooperation. A number of states, it continues, are exploring purchase of some missile defense capability under the Foreign Military Sales program.

The BMDR Report declares that the goal of renewing cooperation with Russia on missile defense is receiving special emphasis, but without negotiating constraints on future U.S. BMD capabilities. One purpose of political dialogue, it states, is to convince Russia's leaders that better U.S. regional missile defenses are needed for reasons of international security and do not pose a threat to Russia's nuclear deterrent posture. An attractive feature of the European PAA, it continues, is that it allows for a potential Russian contribution—for example, early warning radars—if politically feasible.

The United States, it states, is pursuing a close dialogue with Russia on such issues as a joint assessment of ballistic missile threats and a new approach to strategic stability that integrates offensive and defensive capabilities in the hope of producing deeper nuclear reductions by both countries. In addition, the BMDR Report states, the United States is pursuing diplomatic engagement aimed at convincing China that its nuclear deterrent posture is not threatened by U.S. missile defense efforts. But it further states that China must understand that the United States will work to defend its Asian allies and partners from all regional ballistic missile threats. The future, it judges, requires a substantive and sustained dialogue with China focused on enhancing confidence, improving transparency, and reducing mistrust on strategic security issues.

Managing the Missile Defense Program. In its final section, the BMDR Report addresses the new DOD approach to managing the missile defense enterprise so that effective capabilities are acquired, rigorous testing is accomplished, and programs are affordable. In earlier years, the Missile Defense Agency (MDA) was assigned main responsibility for handling the effort in absence of strong guidance from elsewhere in DOD. During 2007–2008, this practice was altered. DOD created a Missile Defense Executive Board (MDEB) to bring together top DOD senior executives as well as Department of State and National Security Council officials to provide guidance on missile defense. Office of the Secretary of Defense staffs, military departments, Joint Staff, and combatant commands were provided authority to influence preparation of the MDA annual program plan and budget submission. In addition, a Ballistic Missile Defense System (BMDS) Life Cycle Management Process was created to provide continuing overview of missile defense programs as they transition from MDA to implementation by the military departments. In the context of this strengthened approach to missile defense management by DOD, the BMDR Report addresses four specific questions:

- What more can or should be done now to strengthen the testing program?
- Can missile defense be made more cost-effective?
- Is internal DOD oversight of the program adequate?
- Is external transparency adequate?

In addressing the testing program, the BMDR Report states that the 2002 approach, which called for simultaneous development and deployment of GBI missiles, was a high-risk acquisition strategy intended to quickly field missile defenses before testing was complete. The new approach, it states, reflects a commitment to fielding proven technologies and missiles. Thus, it urgently requires new testing practices aimed at validating capabilities before they are procured and deployed. Accordingly, it states, MDA is now producing an Integrated Master Test Plan in concert with the Office of the Director, Operational Test & Evaluation, that addresses the testing of each system through the entire development process, rather than looking only 2 years into the future. This plan, it states, outlines a combination of models, simulations, and actual flight tests that can be used to evaluate operational effectiveness and reliability before procurement decisions are made. The new approach to testing and evaluation, it argues, represents a major step forward and addresses concerns, including the need for better metrics for evaluating reliability and performance that arose with the prior test construct.

In addressing cost-effectiveness, the BMDR Report advances key metrics for performance: cost in comparison to other available options, affordability, and the relationship between incurred costs and costs avoided. The BMDR Report thereby implies that missile defense programs will be judged cost-effective if they meet desired performance standards, are less expensive than other options, are affordable within realistic budgets, and help offset costs in such other areas as nuclear forces. But if they fail to meet these criteria because their costs are too high in relation to their effectiveness, they face potential cancellation. Noting that the BMD effort is consuming 2 percent of the DOD budget, it states that the actual life-cycle cost of new missile defense programs is hard to gauge because at early stages, there is no final configuration for the system. As a result, development and procurement costs become variables that depend upon the number of missiles ultimately deployed and their desired performance characteristics. Because of high costs, it states, DOD will not be able to buy enough interceptors to match adversary short-range missiles on a one-for-one basis. This constraint, it judges, enhances the importance of fielding mobile systems that allow missiles to be concentrated quickly in order to address the most immediate threats.

In addition, the BMD Report announces decisions to cancel two troubled programs and to restructure a third:

- The Multiple Kill Vehicle (MKV) has been terminated. Originally intended to equip midcourse interceptors with a capacity to destroy all lethal objects in a threat cluster, the MKV program was terminated because its technology was not maturing well enough and a continuing effort to strive for effective performance was deemed too costly and time-consuming.

- The Kinetic Energy Intercept (KEI) program has been terminated. Originally intended to intercept enemy missiles in the boost-phase of flight, the KEI program was neither affordable nor proven, and its cost had ballooned from $4.6 billion to $8.9 billion, with production costs growing from $25 million per interceptor to $50 million.

- The Airborne Laser (ABL) program was restructured because it had experienced repeated schedule delays and technical problems since inception in 1996, and its operating concept was not adequately defined. Plans for a second ABL aircraft were cancelled, and the first ABL aircraft was shifted to a technology demonstration program.

In addressing internal DOD oversight, the BMDR Report observes that in earlier years, MDA was exempted from DOD standard acquisition rules and the requirements generation process. The new management structure, it states, will correct this problem by bringing multiple actors into the decisionmaking process for missile defense. Stronger internal oversight, it continues, will be provided by the MDEB, by a warfighter-involvement process chaired by U.S. Strategic Command, and by the BMDS Life Cycle Management Process. As a result, the MDA budget now moves through a process that begins with top-level strategic direction, incorporates guidance from the military Services on requirements and desired capabilities, and is subject to final review by the MDEB and Deputy Secretary of Defense. The overall result, the BMDR Report judges, is an improved management process that draws upon MDA's still important strengths in systems engineering and allows other DOD agencies to exert leadership aimed at ensuring that missile defense programs are affordable and meet the needs of the Services and combatant commanders.

In addressing external transparency, the BMDR Report states that earlier MDA special responsibilities and exemption from internal DOD oversight created concerns about congressional oversight and the transparency of missile defense plans, programs, and commitments. To correct this problem, the BMDR Report promises enhanced efforts to keep Congress, committees, and staffs properly informed. This effort, it claims, will include detailed reports on substantive contents typical of all major acquisition programs, numerous special reports per year, and support for Government Accountability Office studies.

Strengths, Shortfalls, and Lingering Issues. The BMDR Report provides the best, most comprehensive DOD analysis of missile defense issues and programs released to the public in many years. Its importance is reminiscent of the famous DOD Damage Limitation Study of 1964, which was a classified study whose landmark contents were publicly released in Secretary of Defense annual posture statements over a period of 4 years. The main effect of the study was to close the door to major BMD deployments because they allegedly were too expensive, too ineffective, and likely to intensify the nuclear arms race. For 35 years after, the United States deployed no missile defenses, trusting nuclear forces to deter nuclear attack. The BMDR Report, in contrast, changes the longstanding U.S. strategic calculus by opening the door to building new but limited BMD defenses that are designed not to protect against Russia's still large nuclear posture, but instead to defend against the smaller, but potentially menacing, offensive missiles of such regional adversaries as North Korea and Iran. Using U.S. missile defense commitments as an important new instrument for achieving greater security in key regions introduces a sea change in U.S. defense strategy, whose implications will take a long time to be fully understood and mastered and will generate a host of technical and strategic issues that will be studied and debated in the coming years. The BMDR Report should be judged in the context of its attractive promises and potent contents, as well as the new and unsettled issues it raises.

Whereas DOD's initial foray into BMD defenses was the 2002 decision to deploy a small GMD posture to protect the U.S. homeland from small-scale missile attacks, the BMDR Report shifts attention away from the GMD posture of 30 ground-controlled interceptors already deployed in

Alaska and California. Instead, it focuses on deploying a larger posture of different missile interceptors that can defend U.S. military forces as well as allies and partners in multiple regions: Europe, Asia, and the Middle East. The centerpiece of this new regional strategy is the SM–3 missile, which originally was intended to protect U.S. warships from missile attack, but now is intended to protect entire countries and regions from enemy missile threats and attacks aimed at cities and other vulnerable targets. The SM–3 program is not the sole beneficiary of the new missile defense strategy, but it is the main beneficiary when judged in strategic and budgetary terms.

The viability of the new strategy depends heavily on anticipated improvements to the technical performance capacity of the SM–3. As many studies have pointed out, the act of employing "hit to kill" technology to shoot down enemy missiles and warheads during their midcourse trajectories is anything but easy; it requires precise hits against targets flying at very fast speed. In recent years, considerable progress has been made on developing the necessary technologies and systems, but as the BMDR Report acknowledges, the current SM–3 Block IA interceptor's capabilities against emerging missile threats are only modest. As a result, the BMDR Report calls for vigorous RDT&E efforts to field successor models. Of these, the Block IB is to be available in 2015 and the more capable Blocks IIA and IIB around 2018–2020. Much depends upon the ability of ongoing RDT&E programs to meet this schedule, but at best, the improved SM–3s are not to be available for 5 to 10 years. Whether this development and deployment schedule will be fast enough to counterbalance adversary efforts to field nuclear-tipped missiles is yet to be seen. Even if this schedule proves adequate, the BMDR Report acknowledges, DOD will face a demanding management agenda to produce improved SM–3s that are effective and affordable. The new DOD management structure seems aligned with meeting this challenge, but only future results will tell.

In gauging the future SM–3 posture, a key issue arises: How many SM–3 interceptors will be needed, how many will be available, and how are they to be fielded? Today, SM–3 interceptors are mounted aboard Aegis warships. Although each Aegis ship can carry multiple SM–3 launchers, currently the Navy has only about 25 such ships in its inventory, and at any given time, only about one-third of them will be deployed abroad. If they are scattered among European, Persian Gulf, and Asian waters, only two to three Aegis warships will be available in each region. To handle this constraint, the BMD Report calls for a mobile practice that relocates these ships in ways that can increase SM–3 concentrations in a single theater to meet the demands of a crisis. But a strategy of rapid relocation means that other theaters could be deprived of SM–3 defenses needed for deterrence and defense in normal peacetime conditions, as well as simultaneous crises. DOD is endeavoring to increase the number of current warships equipped with Aegis radars and launchers, but in future years, construction of additional Aegis ships might be needed—a trend that could bolster arguments for a larger Navy. Beyond this, DOD is proposing to deploy Aegis systems and SM–3 missiles ashore at two sites in Europe. Expansion of this shore-based practice seems likely to spread to Asia and perhaps the Middle East. Moreover, key allies (for instance, NATO Allies in Europe and Japan) are expected to acquire defense missiles of their own—if not the SM–3, then a comparable capability. The future remains to be seen, but when the total number of required SM–3s and other interceptors is added up, the result could be larger missile defense inventories than were foreseen only a few years ago.

Another issue revolves around how much defense capability the future posture of SM–3s and other missile interceptors will provide. Ideally, they should furnish an impregnable roof over regional allies and partners. But the complex physics and mathematics of hit-to-kill practices mean that while numerous enemy missiles can theoretically be shot down, a barrage attack is likely to produce a few that escape and hit their targets. A strong but not impregnable missile defense posture may be potent enough to deter enemy attack in most cases, but most likely, the act of ensuring deterrence in all cases will require a U.S. strategy of still relying upon the threat of nuclear retaliation against aggressors. Indeed, a strategy that relies only upon potentially leaky missile defenses could leave aggressors free to launch missile attacks with impunity, with confidence that they likely will succeed to some degree, and that, in any event, they will not suffer reprisals. As a result, the future likely will yield a U.S. strategy that combines nuclear forces and widespread missile defenses in a setting of proliferating adversary nuclear-tipped missiles. Indeed, some adversaries may enlarge their offensive missile inventories to offset U.S. missile interceptors. Perhaps such an outcome will provide strategic stability, but the BMD Report does not seem poised to ease the transition to a nuclear-free world as envisioned by the Nuclear Posture Review Report. If so, it seems likely to produce a more complex international security system than exists today, one with new dangers of its own.

Yet another issue is whether allies and partners will perform the roles expected of them in the new missile defense strategy. When the decision to cancel the GMD Site Three in Poland and the Czech Republic was announced, several East European and Baltic members of NATO perceived that the step was intended to mollify Russian objections to GMD in Europe. These countries expressed worry, couched in historical memory, that the U.S. decision would leave them exposed to Russian political and military measures. Announcement of the SM–3 PAA for Europe helped quiet these fears and provide reassurance that Europe will be defended against future missile threats from Iran. But while the PAA is intended to form the U.S. contribution to European missile defense, it is expected to be accompanied by complementary missile defense efforts by NATO Allies. At the moment, NATO has its ALTMD concept, but no NATO members have plans and programs to field midcourse interceptors comparable to the SM–3. Appropriate burden-sharing seems likely to mandate European financial contributions to the U.S. PAA. This could require deployment of European defense missiles if the PAA does not provide enough SM–3s to defend the entire continent against future threats. But Europeans face tight budget constraints in ways that could leave them reluctant to spend sizable amounts on missile defenses. If they do not contribute in meaningful ways, the United States could find itself providing missile defense to Europe alone, a development that would add further strains to the already stressed transatlantic relationship.

Similar issues arise in gauging the reactions of allies and partners in Asia and the Middle East.

In Asia, Japan is participating robustly in the U.S. SM–3 program, but South Korea has only begun to consider its requirement for missile defenses, and the same conclusion applies to Australia and other regional allies and partners. The looming prospect is that most of these countries could be threatened by not only Chinese nuclear missiles but also those of North Korea. Defending Europe against new era missile threats from Iran is relatively easy because Europe is small and compact—a modest posture of properly situated SM–3s and other interceptors can provide a protective umbrella over the entire continent. But the Asia-Pacific region is another matter as its island countries are mostly separated by long distances. Short of each country building its own missile defenses or relying on each other for deterrence and defense, protection of this entire vast region will have to be handled mainly by U.S. SM–3 interceptors. While such area coverage by SM–3s may be a manageable proposition for the U.S. military, the act of protecting multiple countries from the same threats raises questions about whether the existing U.S. pattern of purely bilateral treaties with allies can continue to suffice. A collective U.S. missile defense concept could mandate creation of some form of multilateral alliance. So far, enhanced multilateral defense planning has made only initial progress across Asia. Wrestling with the collective and multilateral implications of region-wide U.S. missile defense could become a defining challenge in future U.S.-Asia security affairs.

What applies to Asia holds doubly true in the Middle East and Persian Gulf, where bilateral U.S. security relationships, not collective security, are the dominant pattern. If Iran emerges as a nuclear-armed power in ways mandating U.S.-provided missile defenses across the region, some form of collective multilateral collaboration will be needed. Creating it could be easier said than done.

Finally, how will Russia and China react to a U.S.-led effort to deploy SM–3 missile defenses across multiple regions, including in their own back yards? Thus far, Russia has expressed satisfaction with cancellation of GMD Site Three, and it does not seem to fear an initial SM–3 deployment that will be located in southern Europe and pointed further southward. But if SM–3 radars and interceptors begin appearing in northern Europe in ways that could menace Russian nuclear missiles, the government in Moscow can be expected to react negatively. Under the New Strategic Arms Reduction Treaty (START), the Russians will still have ample nuclear missiles to overpower modest SM–3 defenses. For example, a Russian posture of 700 strategic delivery vehicles and 1,550 nuclear warheads would not be menaced by 100 U.S. SM–3 missile interceptors in Europe. But will this continue to be the case as SM–3 defenses grow in number and capability, even as future U.S.-Russia arms control negotiations strive for deeper reductions in offensive missiles? As the BMDR Report acknowledges, future negotiations will need to address both offensive and defensive forces if stability is to be enhanced. But reaching an accord with Russia may be a difficult task that could compromise the quest for deeper nuclear cuts. A similar judgment applies to future relations with China. Although current U.S. concepts for deploying SM–3 missiles in Asia are mainly focused on protection against North Korea, modest numbers of them could menace China's currently small nuclear posture. Will China react by enlarging its nuclear posture, or will U.S. discussions with China produce a mutual understanding that leaves China's arsenal secure but Asian allies and partners protected from North Korea? Such an understanding is a desirable goal, but whether it can be achieved is uncertain.

CHAPTER SIX

NATO 2020: Assured Security; Dynamic Engagement

Whereas the preceding five chapters do not provide much detailed analysis and guidance on how U.S. overseas alliances should be reformed, this sixth study helps to fill this gap by examining North Atlantic Treaty Organization (NATO) future challenges, prospects, and priorities in considerable depth. *NATO 2020: Assured Security; Dynamic Engagement* (ASDE Report) is a 47-page document released in May 2010. Led by former Secretary of State Madeleine Albright, a multinational team of independent experts wrote it to advise the NATO Secretary-General on how to write a new Alliance strategic concept that would replace the outdated version adopted in 1999. The ASDE Report provides not only advice on the new strategic concept, but also a welter of analyses and recommendations on how NATO as a whole should be reformed to enhance its capabilities for performing old and new strategic missions.

Crafting a Forward-looking NATO Strategic Agenda. While not pretending to offer a crystal ball for predicting where the world is headed, the ASDE Report appraises emerging global security affairs in terms that can be characterized as a blend of guarded optimism and pensive worry. Guarded optimism is appropriate, it judges, because of such positive trends as economic and political progress in Europe and elsewhere, as well as the willingness of many countries to collaborate together to handle common problems. Pensive worry is appropriate, it counters, because of multiple hazardous trends and problems in numerous regions, as well as uncertainty about unpleasant surprises that could lie ahead. The challenge facing NATO, it asserts, is to continue evolving and improving in ways that better equip itself to deal with a fluid, rapidly changing security environment, one that is radically different from the old bipolar structure of the Cold War. In Europe, it states, conventional aggression against the Alliance or its members is unlikely, but the possibility cannot be ignored. The most probable threats to NATO in the coming decade are unconventional: attack by ballistic missiles (nuclear-armed or not), strikes by international terrorist groups, and assaults against NATO's cyber networks. But in a larger strategic sense, it acknowledges, the greatest dangers to Europe's security are arising in the Middle East and other distant regions in ways that compel the Alliance to adopt a broader global outlook.

To deal with this menacing security environment, the ASDE Report urges, NATO should adopt a new strategic concept and associated policies for a two-fold purpose: to assure the continuing security of all Alliance members, and to engage dynamically outside the NATO area to minimize emerging threats. The study sees NATO as a confident and effective but challenged alliance that must muster new types of resolve, cohesion, and capabilities to deal with such new perils as potential troubles with Russia, terrorism, weapons of mass destruction (WMD) proliferation, regional conflicts, and threats to cyberspace and energy security. In the years ahead, it calls upon NATO to perform four basic tasks:

- maintain the ability to deter and defend member states against any threat of aggression
- contribute to the broader security of the entire Euro-Atlantic area
- serve as a transatlantic means for security and crisis management along the entire spectrum of issues facing the Alliance
- enhance the scope and management of partnerships with nonmember countries, international organizations, and other actors.

Accordingly, the ASDE Report puts forth a 15-part strategic agenda for moving NATO toward 2020. NATO, it states, should act by:

- reaffirming NATO's core commitment to Article 5 collective defense missions in ways that shield new and old members from aggression by maintaining adequate military capabilities plus contingency planning, focused exercises, force readiness, and sound logistics

- protecting against such new unconventional threats as WMD attacks, terrorist strikes, and disruption of critical supply lines by updating NATO's approach to defense of security while enhancing the ability to prevail in military operations and broader security missions beyond its borders

- establishing guidelines for operations outside NATO borders in ways that effectively perform agreed-upon missions while reflecting limitations on Alliance interests, scope of external involvements, and resources

- creating conditions for success in Afghanistan by contributing adequately to International Security Assistance Force (ISAF) missions as well as following such principles (there and elsewhere) as cohesion, desirability of unified command, value of effective planning and public diplomacy, aptness of a comprehensive civil-military approach, and need to deploy forces at a strategic distance for an extended time

- employing consultations under Article 4 to prevent or manage crises in ways that share information, promote a convergence of views, avoid crippling disputes, and provide a clear path for successful actions that could be diplomatic, precautionary, remedial, or coercive

- pursuing a new era of partnerships by deepening relationships with existing partners, establishing new partnerships, and expanding the range of partnership activities

- participating in a comprehensive approach to complex problems by being capable of operating in demanding situations that require both military forces and civilian assets, and by collaborating with other countries and organizations that may play lead roles in handling key missions

- engaging with Russia in constructive ways while assuring NATO members that their security and interests will be defended if troubles arise with Russia

- maintaining an open door to potential new members including the Balkan states, Ukraine, and Georgia

- developing new military capabilities for an unfolding era by pursuing transformation and reform, so that future NATO forces can defend their borders, undertake demanding missions at strategic distance, and provide the mobility, flexibility, and versatility needed to be prepared for unpredictable contingencies

- maintaining Alliance-wide solidarity on nuclear weapons policy by keeping secure and reliable nuclear forces for security, employing the Alliance as a whole in making any decisions that alter current deployments or geographic distributions, and supporting global efforts aimed at halting nuclear proliferation

- pursuing the new mission of missile defense by reacting constructively to the U.S. phased adaptive approach (PAA) and jointly carrying out other NATO-wide steps to enhance future capabilities while consulting with Russia and other partners

- responding to the rising danger of cyber attacks by accelerating NATO efforts to respond to such attacks, protect its own communications and command systems, help Allies improve their ability to prevent and recover from such attacks, and develop an array of improved cyber defense capabilities for detection and deterrence

- implementing reforms to create a more agile Alliance by pursuing administrative and other steps aimed at producing a grouping that is leaner, better able to make timely decisions, and more efficient and cost effective

- strengthening NATO's capacity to tell its story to its own population, the entire Euro-Atlantic community, and other regions by widely disseminating the new strategic concept and pursuing other public communications.

Handling NATO Political and Organizational Issues. The ASDE Report states that a new strategic concept offers NATO the opportunity to take stock of recent events and forge a fresh consensus on issues likely to be central to the management and direction of the organization. Those issues are:

- lessons of Afghanistan
- guidelines for missions outside Alliance borders

- administrative reforms
- decisionmaking procedures
- open door policy
- NATO's role in conventional arms control.

In addressing the lessons of Afghanistan since NATO assumed ISAF leadership in 2003, the ASDE Report states that although ISAF has achieved much, its experience has led to concerns within the Alliance about unity of command, restrictions or caveats placed on use of troop contributions by some members, tactics and goals, and civilian casualties. Key lessons learned are:

- NATO must be able to deploy units that are tailored to specific and sustained operations at a distance beyond Alliance borders.
- To the maximum extent feasible, NATO forces should operate under a unified chain of command.
- The need to shield civilians must continue to be emphasized in training and field operations.
- Prisoners and detainees should be treated in accordance with international law.
- Stability in Afghanistan will not come through military means alone: as with other counterinsurgency situations, it requires a civil-military approach that enables local government to earn the trust and loyalty of the population, works closely with partner organizations, and provides help for host-nation security forces.

In addressing guidelines for operations outside NATO borders, the ASDE Report states that while NATO should be firm and resolute in the use of force and related security actions, it should be cautious about undertaking missions not truly necessary and careful not to overextend the Alliance beyond its capacities and its internal consensus. Accordingly, it puts forth three recommendations:

- The new strategic concept should include a set of guidelines for informing NATO decisionmaking about undertaking new missions or responsibilities.

- NATO should maintain a level of preparedness and operational tempo that responds to the security needs of its members, thus avoiding both overreach and complacency.
- Through transparency and effective public communications, NATO must strive to attract and maintain public and legislative backing for its operations.

In addressing administrative reforms, the ASDE Report states, a far-reaching reform agenda should be pursued that strengthens the authorities of the Secretary-General, reduces the number of committees and staffs, reduces costs of headquarters personnel, and otherwise streamlines in ways that produce financial savings. In addressing NATO decisionmaking procedures, the ASDE Report points to an inherent tension between an alliance that always strives for unanimous consensus among 28 members before it acts, and the demands of a new security environment that often require prompt action. It judges that the unanimous consensus rule should be preserved for such critical NATO decisions as commitments, budgets, operations, and new members. But it also calls for more flexible rules on less vital decisions, quicker implementation of decisions that reflect an agreed-upon consensus, and predelegation of some authorities to the Secretary-General and NATO military leaders to respond to such emergency situations as missile or cyber attack. In calling for NATO to preserve its open door policy to new members, it states that further enlargement should continue to be guided by such principles as requiring that new members embrace democratic values and NATO's visions, are implementing necessary military reforms to meet NATO standards, and can contribute to security. In addressing conventional arms control, the ASDE Report states that NATO should support revival of the Treaty on Conventional Armed Forces in Europe (CFE) process, which has been stalled by Russian foot-dragging.

Building Partnerships. The ASDE Report declares that productive partnership relationships with other countries and organizations enable NATO to be more vigilant, better prepared to handle threats, smarter in its actions, and more operationally effective when partners contribute resources to common enterprises. The first generation of partnerships, it states, was mainly intended to facilitate entry of new members into the Alliance, and the second was aimed at recruiting partners for operations in the Balkans and Afghanistan. It judges that a shift to recruiting and nurturing more partners for pursuing broader NATO security activities is now needed. Accordingly, it recommends that NATO should:

- maintain Partnership for Peace activities while strengthening use of the Euro-Atlantic Partnership Council for consultations
- strengthen partnership activities with the European Union (EU) in such areas as developing and using common military capabilities, addressing terrorism, cyber attacks, and energy vulnerabilities, and pursuing comprehensive approaches for handling complex operations in distant areas
- enhance institutional links and cooperative security activities with the United Nations (UN)
- preserve already existing close ties with the Organization for Security and Co-operation in Europe (OSCE) while making use of the OSCE's toolbox of soft power assets
- preserve appropriate partnership activities with Russia while ensuring that the security of all NATO members is protected, and strengthen use of the NATO-Russia Council
- strengthen NATO's ongoing dialogue with Ukraine and Georgia on common security issues
- strengthen NATO partnerships in the Mediterranean and Middle East by employing the Mediterranean Dialogue and the Istanbul Cooperation Initiative
- deepen existing operational partnerships with countries outside the Europe-Atlantic area, including Australia, New Zealand, South Korea, and Japan, all of which have contributed importantly in Afghanistan. In addition, look for ways to cooperate with China on common endeavors and strengthen formal ties to such bodies as the African Union, Organization of American States, Gulf Cooperative

Council, Shanghai Cooperation Organization, and Collective Security Treaty Organization.

Strengthening NATO's Forces and Capabilities. The ASDE Report launches its discussion of Alliance defense priorities by pointing out that for several years, NATO leaders have been calling for steady force improvements. During this time, they have endorsed the Defense Capability Initiative (DCI) of 1999, Prague Summit declaration of 2002, Comprehensive Political Guidance (CPG) of the Riga Summit in 2006, and Strasbourg-Kehl Summit declaration of 2009. All of these proclamations called upon NATO and its members to strengthen forces and capabilities for new missions including expeditionary operations outside Europe. For example, the DCI encouraged NATO force enhancements in five broad areas such as mobility and the ability to deploy, the Prague Summit expanded the list to eight categories and created the new Allied Command Transformation (ACT) and NATO Response Force (NRF), and the CPG called for NATO's land forces to be 40 percent deployable and for 8 percent to be deployable on a sustained basis (the targets were later raised to 50 percent and 10 percent, respectively).

Despite this drumbeat of official encouragement, the ASDE Report declares, NATO forces have improved only slowly, with the result that a significant gap still exists between the requirements of potential missions and actual capabilities. The principal cause for this slow progress, the ASDE Report argues, has been the lack of adequate European defense spending. Today, it states, European defense budgets average well below 2 percent of gross domestic product (GDP) (a standard suggested by many leaders). Only about a dozen members have met goals on their ability to deploy and sustainment. And because most defense budgets are consumed by spending on operations and personnel, not even half of NATO members meet the official benchmark of allocating 20 percent of budgets to investment and procurement. Although encouraging progress has been made by some countries such as Great Britain and France, the predictable result has been a slow crawl toward the future.

To encourage faster improvements, the ASDE Report calls on the new strategic concept to be accompanied by an agreed upon set of priorities for improved capabilities and military reforms. In the coming years, the ASDE Report declares, NATO will need a flexible, deployable, networked, and sustainable military posture that can meet the full range of Alliance responsibilities at affordable cost. NATO's future military posture will need to be capable of performing four central missions:

- deter, prevent, and defend against any threat of aggression in order to protect the political independence and territorial integrity of all Alliance members in accordance with Article 5

- cooperate with partners and civilian institutions to protect the treaty area against unconventional security challenges (for example, cyber attack)

- deploy and sustain forces for expeditionary operations beyond the treaty area when required to prevent an attack on NATO or to protect the legal rights and vital interests of Alliance members

- help shape a more stable and peaceful international security environment by enhancing partner interoperability, training partner military and police forces, coordinating military assistance, and cooperating with the governments of key countries.

If NATO is to fulfill these four missions, the ASDE Report argues, it must halt the decline of defense spending, implement new reforms and efficiencies, and set priorities for future capabilities. To strengthen NATO conventional forces and capabilities, the ASDE Report calls for the following steps:

- provide members reassurance of Article 5 commitments through enhanced contingency planning, preparations for crisis management, equipment assessments, and appropriate military exercises

- achieve ability-to-deploy and sustainability goals by restructuring more forces away from traditional fixed territorial defense missions and creating better strategic lift

- broaden the role of the NRF to perform both Article 5 and non–Article 5 missions
- capitalize on the commonality of Article 5 and expeditionary missions by improving capabilities that can be employed in both
- strengthen command, control, communications, computers, intelligence, surveillance, and reconnaissance (C^4ISR) architectures and information networks
- strengthen special operations forces and capabilities
- upgrade ACT by giving it a bolder mandate, greater authorities, and more resources in order to guide force transformation
- improve education and training
- enhance maritime situational awareness around NATO's periphery, the High North, Persian Gulf, Indian Ocean, and other areas.

Defense reforms and efficiencies, the ASDE Report states, will be needed to make effective use of scarce resources, acquire new capabilities, and combine the often separate defense efforts of many countries. It declares that NATO should encourage:

- new, truly multinational formations with unified command and control, interdependent logistics, and integrated civil-military components
- new informal pooling arrangements, especially for strategic lift
- increased common funding and interoperability for C^4ISR
- common approaches to logistics
- further evolution and coordination of national specialization and niche capabilities
- exploration of opportunities for additional multinational procurement programs
- development of a NATO/EU defense capabilities agency
- use of common funds for costs for selected deployments, including an annual NRF exercise

- further review of NATO's command structure to reduce costs while enhancing force flexibility and ability to deploy.

To strengthen capabilities for common approaches that employ military and civilian assets, the ASDE Report recommends that NATO should:

- prepare at all levels to be part of integrated civilian-military missions
- maintain up-to-date memoranda of understanding with the UN, EU, OSCE, other regional bodies, and nongovernmental organizations
- identify civilian capabilities to be deployed along with combat forces for stability operations
- ask members to identify a cadre of civilian reservists with experience in complex operations that could be deployed when needed
- help partners improve their capacity to contribute to complex operations and comprehensive approaches.

In addressing policies for nuclear weapons and arms control, the ASDE Report states that the Alliance should be prepared for in-depth consultations on the role of nuclear weapons in its deterrence strategy. These consultations should take into account the growing roles of other capabilities as well as the desire to negotiate deep reductions in nuclear weapons. The ASDE Report offers several parameters for consultations and recommendations:

- As long as nuclear weapons remain a reality in international relations, NATO should retain a nuclear component to its deterrence strategy, but at the minimum possible level.
- Currently, the retention of some U.S. forward-deployed nuclear weapons in Europe reinforces extended deterrence and collective defense.
- Broad participation by nonnuclear Allies is an essential sign of transatlantic solidarity and risk-taking—for example, by hosting nuclear deployments on their territory.
- NATO should continue to ensure the absolute physical security of nuclear weapons stored on European soil.

- There should be ongoing dialogue with Russia on nuclear issues, including negotiations aimed at reducing or eliminating substrategic nuclear weapons.

- NATO should reestablish the Special Consultative Group on Arms Control to facilitate its internal dialogue on key issues.

- NATO should endorse a policy of not using or threatening to use nuclear weapons against nonnuclear states that are party to the Non-Proliferation Treaty and its provisions.

In addressing future missile defenses, the ASDE Report endorses the U.S. PAA, and states that NATO should recognize territorial missile defense as an essential Alliance mission. It calls for NATO to agree to expand its ALTMD system to provide the core command and control capability for a NATO territorial missile defense system. It does not specify whether, and to what degree, European missile interceptors should be acquired to complement the U.S.-provided SM–3 missiles.

In addressing how NATO should prepare to respond to unconventional dangers, the ASDE recommends that:

- NATO's Defense Against Terrorism Program should be expanded beyond technology-related work to include research on investigative techniques, deterrence, and social networking.

- NATO should strengthen its efforts and capabilities to defend against cyber attacks.

- NATO should give thought to how to respond to energy supply disruptions in order to mitigate harm to its members and to find alternative sources of supply.

Strengths, Shortfalls, and Lingering Issues. By presenting a comprehensive and detailed analysis of future NATO security challenges and priorities, the ASDE Report fulfills its mandate to provide NATO constructive, usable guidance on how a new strategic concept should be written. It also provides a host of good ideas for shaping NATO plans and programs in the years following adoption of a new strategic concept. It is especially strong in its efforts to identify future Alliance tasks and missions, to call for renewed efforts to protect members in exposed regions, and to urge improvements in NATO conventional forces and capabilities for expeditionary missions. In addition, it correctly calls for focused attention on new threats such as cyber attack and terrorism, improved assets for comprehensive approaches to complex operations, accelerated cooperation with old and new partners, and serious NATO pursuit of defense reforms and efficiencies. All of these strengths make the ASDE Report one of the best NATO studies to emerge in recent years. It ratifies the practice of assembling a team of outside experts to conduct a detailed appraisal of strategy challenges and priorities before U.S. Government and Allied officials begin making official decisions on them, and it provides a model for how U.S. goals and priorities in other regions can be addressed in comprehensive, thorough ways.

Events since its publication show that the ASDE has achieved a major success because many of its analyses and principles were adopted when the Alliance issued its new strategic concept of "Active Engagement, Modern Defense," along with an official communiqué, at the Lisbon Summit in November 2010. Together, the two documents call upon NATO to perform three core security tasks in the years ahead: collective defense of members, crisis management in the Euro-Atlantic area and beyond, and cooperative security by working closely with other allies and partners outside Europe. To carry out these tasks, the two documents state that NATO will:

- keep as its highest priority ISAF success in Afghanistan, transition to full Afghan responsibility and leadership during 2011–2014, and withdraw gradually and only upon proper conditions

- remain steadfast in its commitment to regional stability and security throughout the Balkan region including Kosovo, continue to perform such operations as *Active Endeavor* in the Mediterranean and *Ocean Shield* off the Horn of Africa, and support the African Union in Somalia and elsewhere and the NATO Training Mission in Iraq

- work closely with the UN and OSCE and strive to strengthen its partnership with the European Union

- remain open to new European members that meet Alliance standards, including such candidates as Macedonia, Montenegro, Bosnia and Herzegovina, and Georgia, and continue pursuing close partnership activities with Ukraine and other countries

- pursue a revitalized strategic partnership with Russia in areas of mutual interest and reciprocity

- strive to strengthen its cooperative partnerships with the Euro-Atlantic Partnership Council, Partnership for Peace, Mediterranean Dialogue countries, and Istanbul Cooperation Initiative countries

- continue to promote arms control through such efforts as New START, the Nuclear Non-Proliferation Treaty, and the CFE Treaty Regime.

The two documents also establish important goals and principles for guiding NATO defense planning in the coming years:

- NATO's future military forces should be capable of performing all Article 5 missions and carrying out expeditionary operations outside Europe.

- NATO will pursue reforms, modernization, and transformation toward creating a more effective, efficient, and flexible Alliance so its taxpayers get the most security for the money they invest in defense.

- NATO's military command structure and agencies will be streamlined to conserve manpower and funds.

- Deterrence based on conventional and nuclear capabilities remains a core element of NATO strategy: the Alliance does not consider any country to be an adversary, but no country should doubt NATO resolve if the security of any member is threatened.

- U.S. strategic nuclear forces, supplemented by those of Great Britain and France, provide the supreme guarantee of Alliance security, and NATO will remain a nuclear power for as long as nuclear weapons exist.

- While the threat of conventional attack on NATO territory is low, it cannot be ignored, and Alliance forces must be capable of performing missions to defeat all forms of attacks and threats.

- NATO will maintain the capacity to conduct and sustain concurrent major joint operations and several smaller operations for collective defense and crisis response at strategic distances.

- NATO will develop and maintain robust, mobile, and deployable conventional forces to carry out both Article 5 missions and expeditionary operations, including with the NRF.

- NATO will carry out the necessary training, exercises, contingency planning, and information exchanges for providing viable reassurance and reinforcement for all Allies.

- NATO will ensure the broadest participation of Allies in collective defense planning in nuclear roles, including peacetime basing, C^3I systems, and consultations.

- NATO will develop ballistic missile defenses against future threats by expanding the ALTMD to protect European countries and welcoming the U.S. PAA as an important contribution to meeting missile defense requirements.

- NATO will develop improved capabilities for defending against chemical, biological, and radiological/weapons of mass destruction threats, cyber attacks, terrorism, and threats to energy security and supply lines.

- NATO will develop doctrine and capabilities for expeditionary operations, including counterinsurgency, stabilization, and reconstruction operations as well as better civilian assets for comprehensive operations involving other partners and institutions.

- NATO will sustain the necessary level of defense spending so that its armed forces are sufficiently resourced.

- To use available resources effectively and efficiently, NATO will maximize the deployment capacity of its forces, undertake efforts to meet usability targets, reduce duplication and redundancy, focus development of capabilities on modern requirements, develop and operate capabilities jointly, and preserve and strengthen common capabilities and standards.

- NATO civilian and military authorities will conduct a review of Alliance military forces, capabilities, improvement priorities, reforms, and innovations that will be ready by the time of Foreign and Defense Ministerial meetings that will be prepared in the coming months.

Overall, the new strategic concept is a solid and workmanlike document that does a comprehensive job of identifying most key issues, establishing clear goals, and articulating future policies. Critics are likely to accuse it of being so lofty, general, and abstract that it papers over unresolved issues and controversies (for example, future tactical nuclear warheads in Europe, realistic prospects for cooperation with Russia, strategy for dealing with a nuclear-armed Iran, and willingness to launch future Afghanistan-like operations). While some of these criticisms may have merit, it is fair to conclude that the new strategic concept establishes a solid planning framework whose many details will now need to be decided in future months and years. The bottom line is that the new strategic concept will succeed only to the extent that it is actually implemented, and doing so promises to be challenging. The new concept is best seen as an indispensable part of the solution, but not the whole solution.

Similar conclusions apply to the principles established by the new strategic concept for guiding future NATO defense planning and preparations. Individually and collectively, all of them make sense. But they are long on generalities and short on specifics. While they establish abstract goals, they provide almost no guidance on such critical issues as:

- the extent to which existing NATO defense capabilities are either adequate or inadequate
- the degree to which enhanced capabilities in multiple areas must be built
- required targets for defense spending, investment budgets, manpower, and force levels
- the specific planning and programming agendas that NATO militaries should be pursuing over the coming decade
- how modernization and improvement priorities are to be set in a period of austere budgets

- how NATO and European force structures should pursue innovations, including multinational forces, pooled assets, and common procurement programs, in the future.

The lack of attention to these concrete issues, and the abstract nature of the defense principles put forth by the new strategic concept, owe partly to the decision of the Lisbon Summit to refrain from issuing a special communiqué on defense planning. Such communiqués were issued by three NATO summits over the past years: the Defense Capabilities Initiative of 1999, the Prague Capabilities Commitment of 2002, and the Comprehensive Political Guidance of 2006. All three of these provided the type of detailed defense guidance lacking in the Lisbon Summit and new strategic concept. The task of remedying this deficiency has been handed to NATO defense ministers and foreign ministers in subsequent meetings. In the intervening period, NATO civilian and military officials will have a great deal to consider as they shape the specific defense agenda of the coming decade.

While much will depend upon official guidance emanating from NATO Headquarters, much also will depend upon the defense budgets and improvement efforts pursued by European countries. As the ASDE Report acknowledges, Alliance military forces and capabilities currently are deficient in multiple ways when judged in relation to the requirements and missions facing them in coming years. European defense spending is too low, too few forces are capable of deploying outside their borders, critical enablers are lacking, modernization programs are too slow, and reform efforts are far from complete. The austerity budgets now sweeping over Europe, moreover, are raising the prospect of worrisome cutbacks in spending and forces. For example, Britain recently announced a future 8 percent reduction of its defense budget and 10 to 15 percent cutbacks in its combat forces, the Netherlands has announced a 16 percent cut in its force posture, and Germany has announced a 13 percent reduction to its defense budget by 2015 and a 25 percent reduction to its military manpower. Other countries seem likely to follow suit. The ultimate outcome of this downward trend remains to be seen, but if it spirals out of control, NATO could find itself hard-pressed to fund adequate budgets, perform key missions, acquire vital new capabilities, and modernize and transform its forces at an appropriate rate. In the extreme case, NATO's military strategy and capability could become stuck in a stall pattern—that is, still able to perform old continental defense missions, but no better able to protect the Baltic states and other new members, deploy missile defenses, perform demanding expeditionary operations outside Europe, or pursue comprehensive approaches in unstable areas.

As worried observers are pointing out, such a defense stall pattern could have larger political consequences across the Alliance. The combination of anemic defense efforts, crippling cutbacks in budgets and forces, premature withdrawal from Afghanistan, and unwise decisions to remove U.S. nuclear weapons from Europe could produce not only lowered strategic horizons in Europe but also growing American doubts that the Europeans are willing to carry their weight in Europe and in modern-era security affairs. The interaction of doubtful Americans and inward-looking Europeans, in turn, could erode the transatlantic bond, damage Alliance cohesion, and produce a weakened NATO that is less able to defend Europe, much less play a weighty role in the Middle East and other endangered regions. Such dire consequences are not inevitable, but the key point is that in the emerging situation, they are becoming possible.

Can such a disastrous outcome be avoided? Can the Alliance ensure that the Lisbon Summit and the new strategic concept produce more than fine sounding rhetoric that is not acted upon? Part of the solution can be found if NATO members avoid damaging cutbacks to their defense budgets. The defense budgets for most members are already so small that they are "austerity budgets." Major cuts to them would risk slashing muscle, not just fat. Rather than cutting them unilaterally in large ways, a better practice is to adopt a coordinated multilateral approach, and if some programs are cut, to channel the savings into high priority improvement areas. Once the current emphasis on austerity has passed and sustained GDP is reestablished across Europe, perhaps NATO members can begin restoring real growth to their defense budgets. If so, austerity may become a brief phase that gives way to better funding later in this decade.

Damaging cutbacks to NATO military forces also should be avoided. The Alliance may not need its current posture of 2.1 million European military personnel on active duty or a full gleaming inventory of new weapons. But it needs enough flexible, mobile, deployable forces to handle two major contingencies and several minor ones. Because current military forces can provide only about one-half of this capability, improvements to NATO expeditionary forces and capabilities are badly needed. Fortunately, this agenda is affordable because the necessary enabling assets (better interoperability for joint operations, training and exercise regimes, C^4ISR systems, strategic lift, and logistic support) are not highly expensive. They can be funded if room is made for them in European defense budgets and investment budgets. Over a period of 10 years, a large number of improvement programs in these areas could be funded if only about 5 percent of total European defense spending annually is devoted to them.

In addition to pursuing such programs, NATO will need to take care that it preserves enough high-quality combat forces in the face of potential manpower cuts now under way. On the surface, European members of NATO currently field large forces: their 2.1 million active military personnel generate a huge posture of 165 ground brigades, 2,685 fighter aircraft, and 196 naval combatants. But many of these forces come from Southern Europe and new members in Eastern Europe, and are not well trained or properly equipped for deployment missions. Deployable forces come mainly from Europe's premier, most modern forces—those of Great Britain, Germany, France, Italy, the Netherlands, and a few others. Together, these forces total 40 ground brigades, 1,220 fighter aircraft, and 136 naval combatants.

Judged in relation to potential deployment requirements, this is not a huge posture with plenty to spare. For example, the bulk of these forces could be required if two demanding simultaneous contingencies are encountered (for example, preparedness for defense of the Baltic states against Russia and a major stability operation in the Middle East that requires a sustainable presence). The existing posture, plus U.S. forces deployed in Europe, may be large enough to meet such requirements. But if such key countries as Great Britain, Germany, and France reduce their manpower and forces too far, the outcome could be a smaller posture that is no longer large enough to meet Alliance needs. Maintaining a sufficient posture of modern deployable forces, while improving them qualitatively, should be a central focus of future NATO defense planning even in the face of tight budgets.

In addition to funding expeditionary forces and improvement capabilities, NATO should pursue the reforms and efficiencies endorsed by the ASDE Report and the new strategic concept. Because NATO is a large alliance of many sovereign nations, most of which still plan their defense efforts on a national basis, it does not have a stellar reputation for being efficient and effective in how it applies scarce resources. But much could be accomplished by pursuing common acquisition programs and pooling arrangements, emphasizing niche areas and role specialization, strengthening and enlarging multinational formations, fostering multinational logistic support, and trimming excess or redundant assets. An encouraging step in the right direction has recently been taken by the signing of a British-French cooperation agreement, which calls upon the two countries to create a joint expeditionary force, share use of their aircraft carriers, and jointly develop weapons systems and technologies in the coming years. A broadening of this agreement to include other nations, or the signing of similar agreements by other countries on a bilateral basis, could greatly expand the scope of multinational collaboration across Europe in both funding acquisition programs and generating usable forces. The Lisbon Summit communiqué and the new strategic concept recognize the possibilities and potential for enhanced multilateral cooperation in such areas. The challenge facing NATO and the Europeans is to act vigorously on the idea of multilateral cooperation, for it may be key to the Alliance remaining a potent force in world affairs.

CHAPTER SEVEN

Leading Through Civilian Power: The First Quadrennial Diplomacy and Development Review

A product of an intense study launched by Secretary of State Hillary Rodham Clinton during 2009–2010, the Quadrennial Diplomacy and Development Review (QDDR) Report is the Department of State's first attempt to appraise its strategic goals, internal operations, and resource management efforts in the lengthy, full-fledged manner done by the Department of Defense for its Quadrennial Defense Review Report. For this reason alone, the QDDR Report is a landmark accomplishment, regardless of how its many specific judgments and reforms are appraised. Going back 20 years and more, previous administrations regularly published detailed defense reports on military issues, but none of them offered comparable analysis of the State Department and related diplomatic tools in an era when the demands facing U.S. diplomacy were changing and growing. A step in the right direction was taken by Secretary of State Condoleezza Rice's report, *Transformational Diplomacy*, in the previous Bush administration. Building on these and other efforts, the QDDR Report goes a long way toward closing a still existing wide gap, thus offering readers a powerful tool for judging how U.S. diplomacy and development efforts are intended to work alongside defense efforts in the quest for protecting U.S. security interests and advancing other strategic goals.

A main strength of the QDDR Report is its penetrating treatment of the complex interplay between U.S. diplomatic operations and development endeavors, along with associated crisis prevention and response missions, in such troubled regions as the Greater Middle East, South Central Asia, and others with fragile states that are a breeding ground for violence and terrorism. Beyond question, successfully handling this interplay is centrally important to contemporary U.S. foreign policy and, indeed, to the ongoing U.S. interventions in Iraq, Afghanistan, and other troubled countries. In addition, the QDDR Report pays attention to such important new-era issues as the global economy, energy, climate change, and multilateral activities. In virtually all of these areas, the QDDR Report largely focuses not on substantive policies, but instead on the internal structure and operations of the State Department, U.S. Agency for International Development (USAID), and interagency community, and it puts forth many constructive reform measures. The result is a clear, detailed sense of how the State Department and USAID should evolve and improve in these critical areas.

At the same time, the QDDR Report suffers from its lack of in-depth discussion of substantive policies in several key areas, thus producing a document that does an excellent job of looking inward, but not a comparable job of looking outward in all critical directions or of setting priorities among demanding goals and missions. An additional problem is a lack of material regarding how the State Department intends to form concrete political and diplomatic approaches for handling traditional diplomatic missions that are producing fresh challenges and for carrying out associated guidance on key strategic policies issued by the 2010 National Security Strategy. For example, the QDDR Report devotes little penetrating attention to handling big power relations and associated geopolitics, such as U.S. relations with China, Northeast Asian security affairs, and Iran's quest for nuclear weapons, or to pursuing alliance reforms in key regions. Although the QDDR Report was not written for such purposes, this drawback means that it falls short of putting forth a comprehensive theory of U.S. foreign policy and associated strategic policies in the coming years. But a well-developed partial theory focused mainly on internal U.S. Government structures and operations for new-era diplomacy and development is far better than no theory at all.

Secretary Clinton's Introduction. The QDDR Report was issued in December 2010, the last of the major administration studies on national security issues, and totals 238 pages counting the executive summary and text. It is a product of an extensive effort to consult not only State Department and USAID officials but also outside experts at home and abroad. The study's broad scope and attention to detail manifest the extent to which many people contributed to the process. In her transmittal letter, Secretary Clinton poses a key question: "How can we do better?" To answer this question, she directed that the QDDR Report should provide a thorough review of U.S. diplomacy and development, the core missions of State Department and USAID. The result, she states, is a QDDR Report that provides a sweeping reform agenda regarding how State Department and USAID are to operate collaboratively together and how U.S. civilian field missions in troubled areas are to be carried out.

Secretary Clinton's central argument is that in order to cope with a changing world, the United States must significantly enhance its civilian power: the combined force of civilians working together across the U.S. Government to practice diplomacy, carry out development projects, and prevent and respond to crises. She further argues that although many different agencies contribute to these efforts today, their work must become more unified, focused, and effective. To achieve this goal, she states that the State Department and USAID must play the lead role by providing a strategic framework and oversight on the ground, and by eliminating overlap, setting priorities, funding effective programs, and empowering U.S. officials. This empowering effort, she continues, begins with the overseas ambassadorial Chiefs of Mission, which now are to function as chief executive officers (CEOs) of multiagency missions and to play a bigger role in Washington policymaking. In addition, she calls for USAID to be reestablished as the world's premier development agency, to focus on core areas of expertise, to pursue innovation, and to develop better ways to measure results. Finally, she announces a host of structural and operational reforms within the State Department, all intended to upgrade its performance in handling new missions and remedying previous weaknesses.

In reflecting her guidance, the QDDR Report is anchored in the premise that State is already successfully handling classical diplomacy and related traditional missions, and that the same positive judgment applies to USAID. Accordingly, the QDDR Report does not address these topics in any detail. Instead, it focuses on new challenges and missions, opportunities for improvement, areas of adaptation, and needs for further efficiencies. With this problem-oriented agenda in mind, the QDDR Report is organized into five chapters:

- Global Trends and Guiding Policy Principles
- Adapting to the Diplomatic Landscape of the 21ˢᵗ Century
- Elevating and Transforming Development to Deliver Results
- Preventing and Responding to Crisis, Conflicts, and Instability
- Working Smarter.

Global Trends and Guiding Policy Principles. In chapter one, the QDDR Report's call for enhanced civilian power and effectiveness reflects the judgment that current U.S. foreign policy is under-resourced in this important arena, and that emerging international trends mandate significant improvements to carry out new forms of diplomacy, development, and crisis management. While not questioning the continuing importance of U.S. military power, the QDDR Report points out that in many ways and places, U.S. foreign policy is carried out either mainly by civilians or by civilians working closely with military forces, as is the case in Iraq and Afghanistan. These civilian efforts typically are led by State Department and USAID personnel, but often involve close collaboration with other government agencies such as the Departments of Treasury, Commerce, Homeland Security, Justice, Agriculture, and Energy. A main challenge, the QDDR Report states, is to integrate such multidimensional civilian activities to form a whole-of-government approach so that they carry out U.S. foreign policy effectively and efficiently in complex, demanding settings. More civilian resources are needed, it judges, but equally important are improvements to attitudes, programs, and procedures so that maximum effectiveness is achieved with available resources. The QDDR Report focuses squarely on identifying effects-producing reforms for meeting this challenge.

Chapter one initiates its analysis by putting forth a strategic perspective that reflects the 2010 National Security Strategy's main judgments regarding global threats, current opportunities, challenges, and future opportunities. The task of advancing U.S. interests, the QDDR Report states, involves ensuring deterrence and defense, preserving alliances, preventing new threats such as terrorism and nuclear proliferation, managing the global economy, and upholding American values. It further argues that:

- New global threats are emerging, including terrorism, violent extremism, economic shocks and disruptions, irreversible climate change, cyber attacks, transnational crime, and pandemics of infectious diseases.

- A new geopolitical and geo-economic landscape is evolving that is creating new centers of influence—for example, China, India, Brazil, and others—that are seeking greater voice, representation, and impact.

- Power is diffusing to a wide range of nonstate actors, including nongovernmental organizations (NGOs) and others.

- Today's world, in many regions, is marked by costly conflicts, armed violence, and weak states.

- The information age has accelerated the pace of international change and produced a new era of connectivity.

To handle these trends, which embody a mixture of opportunity and danger, the QDDR Report puts forth a set of seven broad principles for guiding U.S. foreign policy, diplomacy, and development efforts:

- restore and sustain American leadership so that the United States is strong at home and influential abroad

- build a new global architecture of cooperation that will enable nations to form enduring partnerships for addressing common problems in

all critical regions, including Europe, Asia, the Middle East, South
Asia, Africa, and the Western Hemisphere

- elevate the role of development in U.S. foreign policy and better
integrate the power of development and diplomacy: development will
require a new operational model that maximizes U.S. leverage at
producing broad-based economic growth, democratic governance,
major innovations, and sustainable systems for meeting basic human
needs

- mobilize civil society and business to address common problems, thus
creating partnerships with governments aimed at fostering development

- prevent violent conflict and reduce the growing costs of conflict by
strengthening weak governments and their political leadership,
thereby enhancing stability, peace, and progress in endangered regions

- integrate gender into U.S. diplomacy and development work by protecting and empowering women and girls in U.S. foreign policy
agencies and abroad

- facilitate innovative, flexible, and tailored responses in an age of
uncertainty, thereby enabling the United States to react effectively to
fast-changing problems and opportunities.

Adapting to the Diplomatic Landscape of the 21ˢᵗ Century. Chapter two
begins with a brief narrative asserting that although classical diplomacy—
that is, state-to-state diplomacy among big powers—is still important, the
new diplomatic landscape of the 21ˢᵗ century extends far beyond this traditional province. The new landscape, it argues, includes a more varied set of
actors, including many more nation-states pursuing activist foreign policies
as well as nongovernment actors (such as NGOs) and complex interactions
in multiple arenas far beyond foreign ministries. Effective U.S. diplomacy,
it states, must not only adapt to this new landscape, but also strive to shape
it. As a result, it argues, U.S. diplomacy must be prepared to handle three
new domains: lead demanding global civilian operations and whole-of-
government approaches, deal with transnational forces and emerging centers
of influence by building new partnerships and institutions, and deal with

new networks from the private sector to the private citizen. Handling these three domains, the QDDR Report states, will become core missions of the State Department. Accordingly, chapter two puts forth an ambitious agenda of 90 internal reform measures—for the State Department, Overseas Missions, Foreign Service, and civil service personnel—that is clustered into four sections:

- leading the implementation of global civilian operations within a unified strategic framework
- building and shaping a new global architecture of cooperation
- engaging beyond the nation-state
- equipping our people to carry out all our diplomatic missions.

The QDDR Report's analysis of reform measures to enhance implementation of global civilian operations is focused on two subsections: strengthening the role of Ambassadors as CEOs of multiagency missions; and improving interagency collaboration. It strives to upgrade the role of Ambassadors by taking steps to ensure that the National Security Council, other agencies, and U.S. Government personnel understand their accountability to Chiefs of Missions, engage Chiefs of Missions in interagency decisionmaking in Washington, prioritize interagency experience as a key preparation for service as a Chief of Mission, enhance the training and evaluation of Chiefs of Missions, and foster whole-of-government Embassy teams under leadership of Chiefs of Missions. Its analysis of measures to reform interagency collaboration includes steps to leverage the expertise of other agencies, prepare State Department personnel to operate effectively within the interagency, and enhance the State Department operational effectiveness in managing multiagency missions.

The QDDR Report's analysis of reform measures for better building and shaping a new global architecture of cooperation is clustered into five subsections: structuring the State Department for 21st-century global affairs, deepening engagement with close allies and partners, building relations with emerging centers of influence, building the State Department's capacities to organize regionally and work through regional organizations, and updating the State Department's approach to handling multilateral diplomacy.

Within the first subsection, the QDDR Report offers multiple steps to internally restructure and reform the State Department. Prior to this report, the State Department had, in addition to USAID and the U.S. Mission to the United Nations, a structure of six Under Secretaries, each with separate responsibilities and multiple subordinate staffs, plus 14 smaller offices reporting directly to the Secretary of State. To reform this complex structure, the QDDR Report proposes measures to upgrade and expand the missions and capabilities of three functional Under Secretaries, maintain the Under Secretary for Political Affairs as a repository of classical diplomacy with some new assets for working with other offices, and improve the State Department in other ways. The central aim of these reforms is to preserve the State Department's well-developed assets for performing traditional missions while adding significant assets and organizational muscle for handling a wide spectrum of new-era challenges and responsibilities that range from managing the global economy and dealing with energy issues to addressing such threats as terrorism, cyber attack, and proliferation. The main measures include:

- creating an Under Secretary for Economic Growth, Energy, and the Environment—thus adding environment to this position's portfolio
- creating an Under Secretary for Civilian Security, Democracy, and Human Rights—thus adding security and human rights to this position's portfolio
- expanding the capacities of the Under Secretary for Arms Control and International Security Affairs
- establishing a new Bureau for Energy Resources
- appointing a chief economist for global economic issues as a key element of U.S. foreign policy
- establishing a Bureau for Counterterrorism
- establishing a Coordinator for Cyber Issues

- creating a new Bureau for Arms Control, Verification, and Compliance
- restructuring the Bureau of International Security and Nonproliferation.

Within the second subsection—deepening engagement with close allies and partners—the QDDR Report proposes to strengthen the U.S. Mission to the European Union, create a more systematic trilateral process with key Asian allies, bolster the U.S. commitment to Middle East partners, and strengthen North American institutions and relations with our closest neighbors. In addition, the QDDR Report proposes to work with North Atlantic Treaty Organization (NATO) Allies and partners to develop improved Alliance capabilities, and to use the newly created U.S.–European Union Energy Council to forge stronger transatlantic cooperation on global energy issues. Within the third subsection—building relations with emerging centers of influence—the QDDR Report proposes to strengthen strategic dialogues with these actors, deploy more U.S. personnel to these actors, and shift the U.S. consular presences to engage beyond national capitals. Within the fourth subsection—building regional capacities—the QDDR Report proposes to expand its internal focus beyond bilateral relationships to address regional priorities, elevate U.S. efforts to engage regional organizations, coordinate regional responses in the field by creating regional hubs in key U.S. Embassies, improve communication with regional actors and institutions, partner closely with the Defense Department in key places where U.S. military forces are present, and support such innovative regional initiatives as the Pathways to Progress in the Americas and the Lower Mekong Initiative. Within the fifth subsection—improving multilateral diplomacy—the QDDR Report proposes to strengthen the State Department's Bureau of International Organization Affairs, strengthen the U.S. Mission to the United Nations, and elevate multilateral affairs in regional and functional bureaus.

Chapter two's section on engaging beyond the nation-state begins by declaring that although state-to-state relations remain important, modern U.S. diplomacy requires the State Department to reach out to a broad set of nonstate actors. Such efforts, the QDDR Report asserts, must begin with outreach to civil society in multiple regions and globally. Accordingly, it states, Secretary Clinton is launching a Strategic Dialogue with Civil Society aimed at advancing initiatives in areas where the United States and civil societies share objectives. In addition, this section advances analyses and recommendations in three subsections: public diplomacy, community diplomacy, and 21st-century statecraft. The overall aim is enhancing the State Department's capacities to support the important U.S. foreign policy objective of strengthening engagement not only with foreign governments, but also with their societies and cultures in ways that bolster communication and dialogue, and thereby to expand awareness of American intentions, purposes, and contributions to the common good.

The subsection on public diplomacy announces a roadmap, prepared by the Under Secretary for Public Diplomacy and Public Affairs, that is intended to align public diplomacy with U.S. foreign policy goals in ways that inform, inspire, and persuade foreign publics. As part of an effort to shape the global narrative, this subsection proposes to establish a new Deputy Assistant Secretary in the Bureau of Public Affairs who will oversee global media and outreach and expand media regional hubs to increase official U.S. voices and faces on foreign television, radio, and other outlets. In an effort to strengthen people-to-people relations, this subsection proposes to upgrade American Centers abroad, expand English language training and access to academic opportunities, and invest more in science, technology, and information networking. In an effort to counter violent extremism, this subsection proposes to create, within the State Department, a new Center for Strategic Counterterrorism Communication that will work with other offices and agencies that deal with this mission. In addition, this subsection proposes to establish Public Diplomacy Deputy Assistant Secretaries in all regional bureaus and to perform regular internal reviews aimed at setting proper goals, resources, and priorities for public diplomacy activities.

The subsection on community diplomacy aims at encouraging U.S. diplomats and other personnel to increase their efforts to build networks of contacts with foreign communities and showcase U.S. commitments to common purposes and universal values. The subsection on 21st-century statecraft proposes to use diplomats and modern technologies, such as computer networks and mobile phone networks, to enhance public-private partnerships that link American diplomats and development experts with the business community and civic leaders to advance such common goals as economic growth, public health, climate control, and human rights. In addition, it calls upon the State Department to streamline and improve the process by which public-private partnerships are developed by using the Global Partnership Initiative Office. Both subsections call for U.S. diplomats and other officials to develop improved skills in such outreach efforts to foreign communities.

Chapter two's final section—on equipping U.S. people to carry out all diplomatic missions—focuses on efforts to empower diplomats and other officials with the right tools, resources, and flexibility for performing new missions that require outreach to foreign governments, other actors, and civil society. It begins by noting the importance of developing new policies and procedures for protecting the safety and security of U.S. foreign-based personnel, balancing mission requirements against risks, and expanding the training of U.S. people for dealing with security challenges. It also calls for a streamlining of workloads and reporting requirements so that U.S. officials have greater time to perform their outreach and engagement missions. Finally, it calls for efforts to equip U.S. overseas personnel with improved digital information technologies to accomplish their jobs.

Elevating and Transforming Development to Deliver Results. Chapter three of the QDDR Report proposes to elevate development to become an equal pillar alongside diplomacy and defense as top U.S. foreign policy priorities, and to improve the process by which U.S. development policies are crafted and implemented so that better results are achieved. Fostering development, it argues, is a strategic, economic, and moral imperative because it offers a way to build an inclusive and prosperous global economy, strengthen failing states and combat violent extremism, encourage democracy and human rights, and acquire larger numbers of reliable, capable partners that can assist the United States in its strategic endeavors. Consistent with prior administration decisions that created the first U.S. national development policy since 1961, the QDDR Report calls upon U.S. policies to focus on several areas where they can deliver meaningful results: food security, global health, global climate change, sustainable economic growth, democracy and governance, and humanitarian assistance while also elevating and redefining the approach to women and girls. To achieve results in these areas, it calls for vigorous development efforts by the U.S. Government that employ partnerships with domestic philanthropists and private remittances, foreign governments, multinational agencies, and corporate businesses. Such partnerships, it argues, can help add leverage to the limited U.S. development budgets that will be available in the coming years. Accordingly, the QDDR Report puts forth an agenda of change, reforms, and greater energy and effectiveness in four sections:

- focusing U.S. investments
- seeking high-impact development based on partnerships, innovation, and results
- building USAID as the preeminent global development institution
- transforming the State Department to support development.

Chapter three's section on focusing U.S. investments calls attention to three already launched administration initiatives as examples of how development efforts can be properly targeted: the Global Hunger and Food Security Initiative—Feed the Future (FtF), the Global Health Initiative (GHI), and the Global Climate Change Initiative (GCCI). Whereas FtF seeks to increase food supply in impoverished regions, GHI seeks to strengthen public health and reduce disease, and GCCI seeks to make low-emission, climate-resilient sustainable growth a key U.S. diplomatic priority. Building on these initiatives, the QDDR Report seeks additional ways to hone U.S. comparative advantages in economic growth, democracy and governance, humanitarian assistance, and empowering women. Fostering sustainable economic growth, it states, is the single most powerful force for eradicating poverty and expanding prosperity, and is best achieved when governments are committed and accountable, and can be motivated to encourage entrepreneurship, spend capital wisely, invest in infrastructure and education, and expand trade. The challenge facing U.S. diplomacy and development policy, it states, is to encourage governments to pursue this path in ways that already have occurred in such countries as South Korea and Taiwan, which have transitioned from relative poverty to sustained growth and prosperity. In addition, the QDDR Report states, efforts to promote democracy and effective governance in responsive regions, provide humanitarian assistance to help alleviate emergencies and disasters in places such as Pakistan and Haiti, and promote gender equality by empowering women are important to helping underdeveloped countries not only to pursue economic growth, but also to achieve capable representative government and build modern civil societies. In all of these areas, the QDDR Report states, the United States can help achieve these critical goals, but its development policies must be focused wisely and effectively so they achieve their desired results.

Chapter three's section on seeking high-impact development judges that although past U.S. assistance has done considerable good across the world, the United States has too often focused on delivery of services rather than on producing systemic changes in the economies, governments, and societies being assisted. Accordingly, it calls for U.S. assistance to transform the ways in which it does business by shifting emphasis from aid to investment with more emphasis placed on helping host nations build sustainable systems of growth and development, and by crafting multiyear plans aimed at having cumulative impacts over the long term. A key element of this new strategy is to strengthen U.S. partnerships with host nation governments, other public and private donors that include 56 nations and 260 multilateral aid organizations, local implementers, the U.S. interagency community, and U.S.-based organizations. Another element of the strategy is to foster innovation as a key engine of economic growth by promoting new discoveries and scientific breakthroughs, by using new State Department and USAID offices for innovation in science, technology, and research to seek game-changing solutions to specific development problems, to increase research funds for high-risk, high-reward projects, to invest in promising new technological programs, and to leverage the assets of the full Federal science community to find solutions to the next generation of shared development challenges. A final element of this strategy is a strong focus on achieving positive, concrete results by strengthening monitoring and evaluation and fostering greater predictability and transparency.

Chapter three's section on building USAID to become the preeminent global development institution acknowledges that over the past 15 years, USAID, which reports to the Secretary of State, has lost much its autonomy, many of its resources, and some of its key talent, all of which have conspired to diminish its operational effectiveness. The QDDR Report endeavors to reverse this downslide by rebuilding USAID capabilities so that it can play a leading role in future development efforts. Accordingly, it launches a rebuilding strategy with three elements. The first element calls for strong efforts to build better USAID human capital by hiring more top development professionals as well as experts on evaluation, planning, resource management, research, and innovations. The second element calls for efforts to strengthen strategic capital and operational capacity by establishing better planning capacities, empowering multiyear development planning in the field, improving management of budgets and resources, and improving performance of field offices in delivering new services faster and more flexibly. The third element calls for steps to elevate the USAID voice in interagency deliberations in Washington, DC, in overseas field missions, and with foreign governments and other development institutions.

Chapter three's section on transforming the State Department in order to support development is also anchored in a strategy of three elements. The first element calls for the State Department to pursue "development diplomacy" by using its prowess to proactively support U.S. development policies and activities. The second element calls for measures to build development diplomacy as a discipline within the State Department by fostering development skill sets among its personnel and establishing institutional mechanisms to develop and promulgate guidance on best practices and management of resources. The third element calls for measures to strengthen management of foreign assistance budgets and eliminate fragmentation by using a new Office of Foreign Assistance to work with senior State and USAID officials to review budgets, analyze new proposals, and allocate resources among programs in ways that produce better strategic planning and enhanced cost effectiveness.

Preventing and Responding to Crisis, Conflict, and Instability. Chapter four asserts that handling fragile states with weak or failed governance, internal conflict, and humanitarian emergencies has become a central security challenge for the United States. It argues that fragile states are often a breeding ground for not only internal violence but also terrorist groups that project their destructive actions outward, as occurred in 2001 when the Taliban government in Afghanistan enabled al Qaeda to gain the foothold that allowed it to attack the United States. For the past two decades, it states, the U.S. Government has recognized the need for an effective approach to fragile states, but has struggled to understand this challenge and organize its civilian institutions to cope with it. It states that while many of the necessary skills and capabilities exist at State, USAID, and other Federal agencies, these assets are not organized and focused to address the problem in sustained, effective ways. Too often, it asserts, U.S. reactions have been post hoc and ad hoc in ways that miss early opportunities for conflict prevention, struggle to organize U.S. responses properly, rely on outmoded strategies and field missions that are not prepared for the task, fail to properly coordinate resources and multiple agencies, fail to work closely with multilateral institutions and foreign governments, and do not cope adequately with unanticipated consequences of interventions. The time has arrived, it judges, for a new U.S. approach that transforms this recipe for failure into a strategy for effective responses and sustained success, one taking into account the likelihood that future operations will differ from those in Iraq and Afghanistan. Building on lessons learned from past failures and successes, the QDDR Report calls for efforts to:

- adopt a lead-agency approach between State and USAID as well as a complementary division of labor and joint operations between them

- bring together a cadre of experienced personnel to fill out a standing interagency response corps that can deploy quickly and operate effectively in the field
- develop a single planning process for conflict prevention and resolution missions in fragile states as well as standing guidance that does not depend on individual Embassies
- create better ways to coordinate civilian and military operations in the field in order to prevent and resolve conflicts, counterinsurgencies and illicit actors, and bring security to local populations
- coordinate and integrate assistance to foreign militaries, civilian police, and justice sectors
- work closely with such partners as host nations, other countries, and multilateral institutions
- strengthen U.S. capacity to anticipate crises and conflicts and to apply scarce resources wisely.

To carry out this agenda, the QDDR Report divides chapter four into three sections:

- embracing conflict prevention and response within fragile states as a core civilian mission
- executing conflict prevention and response in the field
- building a long-term foundation for peace under law through security and justice sector reform.

The first section strives to put forth measures aimed at enhancing U.S. capacity to treat conflict prevention and response as a core civilian mission. It puts forth a five-fold agenda of measures to better define missions, execute missions, reshape State Department structures to fit missions, expand USAID capacity for missions, and pursue whole-of-government approaches. The act of better defining missions, it states, requires recognition that U.S. operations will be required to cope with a wide spectrum of situations ranging from preventing conflict, to resolving conflict and violence, to fostering stability, to engaging in postconflict reconstruction and recovery. The act of better executing such missions, it states, requires a U.S. Government division of labor in which the State Department will lead operations in response to political-security crises and conflicts, and USAID will lead humanitarian response operations. State and USAID, however, will cooperate closely in missions that require involvement from both, and proper leadership and coordinating authority will be delegated to field missions. The act of reshaping the State Department, it states, will require steps to unite departmental capabilities through the Under Secretary for Civilian Security, Democracy, and Human Rights, to create a Bureau for Conflict and Stabilization Operations under the Office of Coordinator for Reconstruction and Stabilization (S/CRS), and to build a stronger Civilian Response Corps. The act of expanding USAID capacities, it asserts, requires strengthening the Office of Transition Initiatives and regional bureaus as well as better staff assets for recovery and stabilization programming and operations. The act of pursuing whole-of-government approaches, it states, requires close civilian-military cooperation, a new International Operational Response Framework, and joint training of civilians in multiple Federal agencies.

Chapter four's section on executing conflict prevention and response in the field calls for creating a better deployable surge capability by upgrading the Civilian Response Corps with an active component that has appropriate skill sets and replacing the unfunded civilian reserve of 2,000 personnel with a smaller "Expert Corps" consisting of a roster of technical experts willing to participate in deployment operations. This section also calls for steps to better organize Embassies and USAID missions for conflict, crisis, and stability operations through better technical training, management skills, security arrangements, logistical support, and flexible use of resources. In addition, this section calls for better use of data and evidence to deliver results through such measures as state-of-the-art knowledge and training, sound operational and strategic guidance, careful measurement of operational effectiveness on the ground, and improved crisis forecasting. Finally, this section calls for improved operational coordination with allies and multilateral organizations, building of better foreign police and military capacities, and modernization reforms for United Nations peace operations.

Chapter four's section on building a long-term foundation for peace under law through security and justice reform argues that if fragile states are to be stabilized, they require better internal security forces and judicial systems capable of maintaining law and order, protecting citizens, and administering justice against criminals. It further argues that although current U.S. capabilities often excel at training foreign militaries and police forces, they lack comparable assets at building judicial systems and rule of law programs. Accordingly, it asserts that U.S. assistance efforts in this critical arena need to be more comprehensive and better integrated in ways that enhance U.S. capabilities, create models for better in-country management, and foster host nation ownership of better security and justice systems.

Working Smarter. Chapter five aspires to improve the efficiency of the State Department and USAID at using scarce resources by proposing reforms to their personnel policies, procurement practices, and planning capabilities. Internally focused on how to shift emphasis from inputs to outputs, it contains four sections:

- building a 21st-century workforce
- managing contracting and procurement to better achieve missions
- planning, budgeting, and measuring for results
- delivering mutually supportive quality services and capturing further efficiencies in the field.

The first section observes that in recent years, demands on State Department and USAID personnel have expanded in order to perform new missions, and that the field presence of both agencies has enlarged significantly in frontline states such as Afghanistan, Pakistan, and Iraq. It argues that shortages in staffs and skills have been growing impediments to meeting new challenges there and elsewhere. Accordingly, it calls for larger numbers of personnel for both agencies, beginning with the 3,000 new Foreign Service and civil service personnel already authorized by Congress. But it also calls for strong efforts to get maximum performance from the workforce by increasing its effectiveness and efficiency. Accordingly, it calls for steps to:

- marshal better expertise to address 21st-century challenges by hiring skilled personnel from outside State and USAID

- reward and better use the civil service by expanding overseas deployment opportunities, create new opportunities for converting to the Foreign Service, and strengthen career pathways for civil service personnel

- close the experience gap in the Foreign Service by tripling midlevel hiring at USAID, create more limited-term appointments for experienced personnel, and prepare surge hires to assume midlevel responsibilities

- recruit and retain highly skilled locally employed staff by establishing a new senior staff cadre and by ensuring that compensation and benefit plans reflect local markets

- train U.S. personnel for new missions by expanding training staffs, pursuing cross-training between State Department and USAID, tying training to promotion, increasing rotation assignments to other agencies and from other agencies to State and USAID, strengthening management training, launching a development studies program, and encouraging interagency training across the U.S. Government

- align incentives and recognize performance by rewarding innovation and entrepreneurship, and by aligning performance tools with new skills and priorities.

The second section notes that as State Department and USAID mission demands have increased, both agencies have resorted increasingly to hiring contractor personnel. To reduce resulting problems, this section calls for measures to balance the State and USAID workforce by relying more on direct-hire employees, elevating the performance of contracting officers, establishing a budget mechanism to fund contracting needs at USAID, using more fixed-price contracts, and establishing better oversight of large contracts. In addition, it calls for steps to increase competition among contractors by using smaller and more focused awards at USAID and to increase small and disadvantaged business participation in foreign assistance contracting. Finally, this section calls for steps to build better local development leadership in this arena by strengthening the contracting capacities of foreign governments, local society, and the private sector.

The third section asserts that in order to use their resources efficiently, the State Department and USAID need an improved planning and budgetary process that allows for sound policy decisions and effective implementation. Important steps already have been taken by creating a Deputy Secretary of State for Management and Resources, which has brought greater coherence to strategic planning and budgeting, and by creating at USAID a new Office of Budget and Resource Management that will enhance that agency's capacity for executing the budget for development programs. As of 2013, it states, USAID will submit a comprehensive budget proposal that will be included in the broader State Department foreign assistance budget. It declares that further reforms are necessary in the following areas:

- elevate and strengthen strategic planning by establishing improved multiyear strategic plans at the State Department and USAID as well as associated plans for regional and functional bureaus and integrated country strategies with diplomatic and foreign assistance components

- align budgets to planning by transitioning to a multiyear budget formulation based on strategies for countries and bureaus

- create better monitoring and evaluation systems aimed at strengthening capacity to develop improved indicators, measure performance, and identify best practices

- streamline and rationalize planning, budgeting, and performance management by creating a coherent process that establishes priorities, translates these priorities into budgets, and provides accountability

- transition to an integrated national security budgeting and planning process by working with National Security Council staff, Defense Department, and other departments and agencies to create whole-of-government approaches in this arena—and use this process to resource changing missions in Iraq and Afghanistan, establish an overseas contingency operations budget, pool funding for common projects, and achieve better budgetary coordination among contributing departments and agencies.

The fourth, final section deals with measures to deliver mutually supportive quality services and capture further efficiencies in the field. It mainly addresses steps to consolidate administrative services and to pursue information technology modernization at overseas posts. It establishes a high-level Administrative Board initially composed of State Department and USAID officials to pursue these aims.

Strengths, Shortfalls, and Lingering Issues. Because the QDDR Report is the first such report on the State Department and USAID, it must be judged on its own merits and unique features rather than in comparison to preceding documents. Owing not only to its length and detail, but also to its comprehensive treatment of many important issues, it makes a large contribution to crafting new approaches for managing the State Department and USAID, and it will serve as a standard bearer for writing future QDDR Reports in ways that complement the Defense Department's QDR Report. When read alongside the QDR Report of 2010, the QDDR Report helps fulfill the administration's mandate of putting forth coherent analyses for determining how diplomacy, development, and defense are to work together to advance U.S. security and strategic interests abroad. It makes a convincing case for its judgment that strengthening U.S. civilian power is critical to carrying out modern-era foreign policy and national security strategy. In reflecting Secretary Clinton's guidance on shaping its contents, it puts forth a sweeping reform agenda for the State Department and USAID that includes many provisions for changes in their internal structures and operations at home and abroad.

While many of its reforms are likely to be appraised as wise and constructive, others may be debated and challenged by critics. Regardless, the QDDR Report is best judged as a whole rather than for its particulars and details. The bottom line is whether the QDDR Report charts a sound path, as Secretary Clinton argues, for enabling U.S. foreign policy to "do better" in future years. Whether it will succeed in this regard is to be seen. Deciding upon internal State/USAID reforms to structures and operations is one thing; fully implementing them so that they work effectively is something else again—and, in key ways, more challenging. As an old slogan holds, the proof of the pudding lies in the eating. Several years are likely to pass before the QDDR's many reforms can be judged on the basis not only of their theoretical soundness, but also, more importantly, on their actual performance. For now, an appropriate conclusion is that the QDDR's reform agenda seemingly is pointed in the right strategic direction.

The QDDR Report makes a strong case for more resources in manpower and budgets for the State Department and USAID. Its argument is fair; in particular, many outside observers have judged that U.S. foreign policy and diplomacy suffer from underfunded budgets, and that more skilled professionals are needed in multiple areas. The political problem, however, is that the era of ever expanding Federal budgets seemingly has passed, as Defense and other agencies are now finding out. The State Department and USAID are likely to be affected by future budgetary austerity in similar ways. If so, this will compel both of them to extract the maximum mileage from the budgets and manpower that will be available—a judgment about the need for efficiency and effectiveness that the QDDR Report shares.

If the QDDR Report is to be criticized on its own terms, its internal focus on reforming structures and operations rather than on outward-looking policies results in a lack of insightful material about the difficult task of setting priorities among new, proliferating State Department and USAID roles and missions. The QDDR Report puts forth a lengthy but abstract and general agenda on overseas goals to be pursued, missions performed, and responsibilities accepted, especially in unstable regions such as the Greater Middle East and South Central Asia. In the process, it does not convey a clear sense of limits and constraints or describe endeavors that must be sacrificed on behalf of other higher priorities. As the report makes clear, the United States will need to pursue demanding activities in its diplomacy, development efforts, and crisis management policies in such regions in the coming years. But, just as clearly, the United States will not be able to handle all potential challenges at once with equal vigor. Priorities will have to be set and frustrating limitations acknowledged. A key question arises: What diplomatic, development, and crisis management goals must be scaled back and activities truncated in their pursuit? Owing to its inward focus, the QDDR Report does not answer this question or even seriously address it, but this does not make the question any less imperative as the future unfolds.

The QDDR Report's effort to restructure the State Department internally reflects the judgment that new and improved assets are needed to handle the rapid proliferation of new missions, responsibilities, and challenges facing U.S. foreign policy and diplomacy. The measures to upgrade several Under Secretaries, to add new bureaus and offices in such areas as foreign economic policy, energy, counterterrorism, and cyber security, and to beef up public diplomacy all arguably make sense. The payoff will be a new State Department that can strongly perform more functions in policy analysis and diplomatic leadership than now, including in areas critical to the administration's national security strategy. The drawback will be a State Department that, already known for its internecine battles and struggles to forge coordinated decisions, is more complex than now—and more challenging to lead. Even more than now, future Secretaries, Deputy Secretaries, and Under Secretaries will have their work cut out for them. A similar judgment applies to the idea of empowering Ambassadors as Chiefs of Missions so that they can better function as CEOs for directing multiagency activities in their countries and regions. This reform is clearly needed, especially in troubled spots where U.S. diplomacy and development require a host of different agencies pursuing distinct agendas plus close cooperation with host countries, partner countries, international organizations, and other actors. The challenge facing future Chiefs of Missions, even if they are empowered, will be to perform this difficult job and juggling act while also maintaining influential positions in Washington policymaking.

The QDDR Report's efforts to strengthen USAID internally, to grant it a newly influential role in forging development policy as part of the State Department, and to make it the world's preeminent development agency respond to the multiregional challenges facing the United States in this critical arena. As these reforms are implemented, time will tell whether USAID evolves along these desired lines and delivers better results than now. An equally important issue is whether, in response to the QDDR Report, U.S. development policy is now pointed in better strategic directions that could produce improved concrete results. The QDDR Report argues in favor of revised U.S. development and assistance efforts focused on making investments rather than on delivering services in ways that help targeted countries and regions to achieve self-sustaining economic growth and political progress, and on achieving high-impact results by working closely with other countries and actors to provide coordinated assistance efforts. This basic development strategy makes sense as a way to get more mileage out of scarce U.S. development and assistance resources and to achieve better collaboration with the plethora of aid efforts flowing from multiple countries, international organizations, and other actors. But the QDDR Report advances this strategy in abstract terms without providing much analysis of how individual regions and countries will be affected in ways that could require differing investment strategies and development agendas. Beyond this, the QDDR Report can be read as seemingly aspiring to ambitious worldwide development goals because it does not discuss specific priorities for U.S. regional strategies and country agendas, not all of which can be transformed overnight or even over many years. This is a shortfall; a better sense of priorities is needed to determine whether future U.S. development policies and strategies will be targeted in wise and effective ways.

The QDDR Report acts sensibly and insightfully in its efforts to elevate the goal of preventing and responding to crisis, conflict, and instability in fragile states to a key imperative of U.S. foreign policy and diplomacy. As it states, the multiplicity and diversity of challenges in this arena, which go beyond Iraq and Afghanistan, require a better planning process and sound strategic guidance for shaping and calibrating U.S. activities in differing places. Keys to this endeavor are the acts of defining and executing missions, achieving close civilian-military collaboration, pursuing whole-of-government approaches, and working with partners in sustained, effective ways. The QDDR's division of labor between the State Department and USAID, with the former leading political-military crisis missions and the latter leading humanitarian assistance efforts, provides a path to deconflicting and harmonizing the activities of both agencies. Of special significance is the QDDR Report's decision to create, at the State Department, a Bureau for Conflict and Stabilization Operations under S/CRS. Also important is the decision to continue building a strong Civilian Response Corps of active personnel, but the accompanying decision to scale back its civilian reserve component to a smaller Expert Corps risks having too few personnel if multiple missions must be performed.

Throughout, the QDDR Report strongly emphasizes the need for the State Department and USAID to do a better job of managing resources. It makes the case for more State/USAID personnel, but it also puts forth an activist agenda for better using existing manpower resources by hiring more skilled experts from outside the two agencies, doing a better job of training, and fostering other improvements to the Foreign Service and civil service. Its measures to improve contracting procedures and to do a better job of relying upon government employees to reduce reliance on private contractors are sound. The QDDR Report also deserves high marks for its emphasis on fostering improvements to strategic planning, multiyear budgeting, and use of output measures and metrics—areas where State traditionally has not been as strong as Defense. Whether the State Department and USAID will succeed in their agenda to better link plans and budgets to personnel and operations is to be seen. The QDDR Report also calls for efforts to do a better job of developing interagency plans for budgets and resources, but progress in this important arena lies mainly beyond its province.

Finally, the QDDR Report suffers from a key shortfall in its failure to address emerging changes to classical diplomacy and the need for the State

Department to pursue internal reforms to deal with them. Possibly because the QDDR Report was not written to address this issue in any detail, it tends to assume that classical diplomacy will be a constant in the future strategic equation and that the State Department is both handling associated challenges effectively and is properly organized for dealing with them. In its first two chapters, the QDDR Report earmarks these challenges, but it discusses them only briefly, and it does not put forth a well-articulated set of policies, strategies, and efforts to deal with them. A strong case can be made, however, that classical diplomacy is a fast-changing variable, not a constant. New challenges are emerging in such areas as handling big power geopolitical relations with Russia and China, creating new regional security architectures, deterring new nuclear powers and other potential rivals, and reforming alliances so that new missions can be performed. In these areas, new types of thinking and calculating will be needed about U.S. foreign policy, the relationship between civilian and military power, and diplomatic goals and strategies. To address this demanding agenda, the State Department may need to address how its Office of the Under Secretary for Political Affairs and its Bureau of Political-Military Affairs are to be staffed, structured, and operated. For both offices, an agenda of reform may be necessary. The QDDR Report's silence does not make this issue any less important.

A Comprehensive Blueprint with Lingering Issues

By any measure, the seven official studies surveyed in the preceding pages are extensive and wide ranging in the issues that they raise and the departures that they promote. Together, they put forth fully 671 pages of analysis for launching the national security strategies and defense plans of a new administration, a total that far surpasses the comparable publications of other incoming administrations for more than the past two decades. All of these studies are excellently written and cogently argued. They succeed in their core task of providing high-level, path-setting guidance to U.S. Government departments and agencies on creating new-era strategic goals and implementing agendas. In the process of providing an unusual degree of transparency, they offer the American people, as well as foreign countries, a great deal of material to chew on and digest. Regardless of whether their key judgments are accepted or rejected, those who read these studies will come away with a better sense of what the administration is thinking and where it proposes to lead the United States and the world.

Each of these seven studies is important in its own right and deserves to be read and evaluated on its individual merits. Equally important, they should be read and judged collectively because they combine to create a comprehensive blueprint for guiding how future strategies, policies, and plans are to unfold in ways intended to be mutually reinforcing and to produce cumulating results. This blueprint is not heavily infused with ideology from either end of the U.S. political spectrum. Instead, it comes across as mostly centrist, pragmatic, and technical in its thinking, but with features that have left some liberals perceiving too much conservatism at work, and some conservatives perceiving too much liberalism. Taken as a whole and judged in strategic terms, this blueprint can help promote bipartisan consensus in the field of national security strategy and defense planning. However, to the extent that it triggers partisan debate, it illustrates the difficulties of building full-fledged bipartisanship in today's polarized political climate.

A Blueprint of Continuity and Change. The seven studies form a comprehensive blueprint because they perform different functions that are designed to interlock in complementary ways. Essentially, the National Security Strategy of 2010 (NSS 2010) provides the political foundations for a new U.S. strategy that employs American economic renewal and a whole-of-government approach as engines for driving an assertive, refocused strategy of engagement abroad. A blend of continuity and change, this new strategy is focused on such top strategic priorities as strengthening homeland defense, defeating al Qaeda and succeeding in Afghanistan, preventing further proliferation of weapons of mass destruction (WMD), making the Middle East more secure, and building improved alliances and partnerships. These are all part of a larger effort aimed at creating a cooperative international order for handling common security challenges. Mainly preoccupied with articulating an integrated set of goals, this new strategy is both hopeful and ambitious. It not only employs multiple instruments, including diplomacy and civilian assets for comprehensive approaches in turbulent places, but it also acknowledges a need for strong U.S. military forces to help achieve national goals in peace, crisis, and war. By providing this political foundation for U.S. national security strategy, the NSS 2010 creates a framework for determining how the five subsequent studies, which mainly focus on military and defense issues, can be incorporated into the comprehensive blueprint.

The Quadrennial Defense Review (QDR) Report aspires to provide a new approach to U.S. defense planning that can serve the new national security strategy. Aimed at pursuing four strategic goals by strengthening U.S. military forces for six high-priority missions, it calls upon the Department of Defense (DOD) to pursue an agenda of rebalance and reform in ways that devote special attention to improving capabilities for current wars while remaining attentive to longer term imperatives. Its top priorities for rebalancing include defending the U.S. homeland, succeeding in counterinsurgency, stability, and counterterrorism operations, building the security capacity of partner states, improving U.S. military capabilities for performing in antiaccess environments, preventing WMD proliferation, and operating effectively in cyberspace. It calls for future U.S. military forces that are flexible and adaptable in ways enabling them to handle a wide spectrum of contingencies, including two concurrent major operations. Although it cancels or scales back several expensive weapons acquisition programs, its reform agenda is focused on making DOD efforts in that area more effective, timely, and affordable.

Although written as a criticism of the QDR Report, the congressionally mandated QDR in Perspective (QDRP) Report is valuable as a complementary contribution because of the heightened attention that it devotes to force-sizing constructs, the need for a larger Navy, long-term modernization of U.S. forces, and vigorous reforms to the weapons acquisition process. It also calls for changes to the interagency process in ways that will enhance strategic planning at the onset of each administration. Together, the QDR Report and QDRP Report in particular provide a framework for judging how U.S. conventional forces should be improved and how new regional security and deterrence architectures are to be built.

The Nuclear Posture Review (NPR) Report complements the QDR Report and QDRP Report by providing a new strategy toward U.S. nuclear forces and preparations. It is focused on preventing WMD proliferation and WMD terrorism, reducing the role of U.S. nuclear forces in national security strategy, maintaining strategic deterrence and stability at reduced force levels, strengthening regional deterrence, reassuring allies and partners, and maintaining a safe and effective nuclear arsenal. As part of a large set of policies for reducing the role of nuclear weapons in U.S. strategy and preventing WMD proliferation, it strengthens already existing assurances that U.S. nuclear weapons will not be used against nonnuclear states that comply with Non-Proliferation Treaty provisions. In addition, it introduces the new and distant goal of ultimately achieving a world without nuclear weapons. For the long period until this goal can be accomplished, the NPR Report is attentive to U.S. requirements for capable nuclear forces at lower levels than now. It endorses the New Strategic Arms Reduction Treaty (START) reduction of U.S. and Russian forces to 700 strategic delivery vehicles and 1,550 warheads and calls for even larger reductions in subsequent negotiations. But it also calls for retaining a sizable triad of intercontinental ballistic missiles, ballistic missile submarines and submarine-launched ballistic missiles, and heavy bombers, for modernizing them in moderate ways and for strengthening management of the nuclear arsenal.

Of the five defense studies, the Ballistic Missile Defense Review (BMDR) Report puts forth the biggest change and newest thinking of all. Rather than continue solely with the Ground-based Midcourse Defense program aimed at defending the U.S. homeland from ballistic missile threats posed by such countries as North Korea and Iran, it proposes instead to broaden the ballistic missile defense effort by deploying significant numbers of SM–3 interceptors to defend regional allies and partners in Europe, Asia, and the Middle East. Judged in historical and strategic terms, this missile defense program is truly a sea-change in U.S. defense strategy with wider implications. The BMDR Report proposes to blend enhanced missile defenses with U.S. conventional forces and nuclear commitments to provide integrated military forces for underwriting efforts to create new security and defense architectures in all three regions. It suggests that as the contributions of missile defenses as well as U.S. and allied conventional forces increase, nuclear forces and commitments can play a reduced role. Consequently, the BMDR Report ushers into existence a new era for U.S. thinking about how best to achieve security and stability in Europe, Asia, and the Middle East.

Whereas all of these defense studies largely focus on U.S. military preparedness efforts, the *NATO 2020: Assured Security; Dynamic Engagement* (ASDE Report) focuses intently on how to energize the defense efforts of North Atlantic Treaty Organization (NATO) Allies in Europe. Written to help advise NATO on how to write a new strategic concept, it calls upon NATO strategic planning to address new-era missions in Europe and distant regions. It proposes a set of changes aimed at enhancing the NATO ability to protect its exposed borders and to defend against such new-era threats as missile attack, terrorism, and cyber attacks. In addition, it calls upon the Alliance to improve its military forces and capabilities for expeditionary missions, embrace comprehensive approaches, and broaden its cooperation with partners from multiple regions. The effect is to give NATO plenty of new ideas and departures to think about as it charts the future over the coming decade.

The Quadrennial Diplomacy and Development Review (QDDR) Report puts forth a lengthy, intensive analysis of how U.S. civilian power should be increased, how diplomacy and development policies in troubled regions should be carried out, and how internal Department of State and U.S. Agency for International Development (USAID) structures and operations should be reformed. Provided it is strongly implemented, it will enhance the capabilities of State and USAID to operate effectively in the coming years. The effect is to give the State Department and USAID a demanding but promising agenda to carry out in future years.

Lingering Issues. The comprehensive blueprint created by the seven official studies leaves lingering issues and controversies in its wake, all of which create reasons for further analysis aimed at resolving them in ways that further strengthen the blueprint while eliminating gaps and inconsistencies:

- The NSS 2010 may be so hopefully ambitious in its global designs that it overly discounts the constraints facing the United States, and fails to adequately treat the risks of potential major power competition. In addition, it fails to address future U.S. strategy in the Middle East if Iran acquires nuclear weapons, and does not provide long-term political and strategic concepts for guiding security affairs in Europe and Asia.

- The QDR Report is so preoccupied with handling near-term priorities that it fails to give full attention to long-term imperatives including

U.S. force requirements, joint operations, and modernization. In addition, its call for creating new regional security architectures seems focused on handling military forces in the absence of larger political purposes and designs.

- The QDRP Report is attentive to long-term force sizing, modernization, and acquisition reform, but it fails to illuminate how a larger Navy and a more ambitious modernization effort are to be funded.

- Although the QDR Report and QDRP Report urge enhanced security assistance for troubled states, they do not provide strategic design concepts for determining how the forces of allied countries in Europe, Asia, and the Middle East are to be improved, made more interoperable with U.S. forces, and integrated to perform common deterrence and defense missions.

- The NPR Report does not provide sufficient analysis of whether its complex approach to preventing further WMD proliferation and nuclear terrorism will succeed. While it provides a viable triad under New START provisions, it does not specify how far additional reductions can be taken.

- The BMDR Report puts forth a new and ambitious strategy for deploying regional missile defenses, but this strategy is highly dependent upon successful SM–3 development programs as well as the willingness of allies and partners to cooperate in the enterprise.

- The ASDE Report articulates an ambitious agenda for improving and reforming NATO, but it was issued before the emerging wave of European defense spending cuts, which will affect how NATO's future is best handled.

- The QDDR Report puts forth an ambitious agenda for U.S. diplomacy and development policies in troubled areas, but it does not set clear priorities in these areas or articulate a new-era agenda for how classical diplomacy is to be carried out.

- All of the official studies on U.S. national security strategy and defense planning assume that adequate budget resources will be available to carry out their future policies and programs. Growing political pressures to reduce Federal deficits partly by cutting expenses are calling this assumption into question. Once firm decisions are made about potential budget cuts to national security programs, careful reviews of these programs and their associated policies likely will be needed. A key bottom line, noted by the NSS 2010, is that sustained growth by the U.S. economy will be critical to carrying out the coming future national security agenda.

Future Analytical Challenges. In addressing these lingering issues, future analyses and studies will be well focused if they include the following topics:

- how U.S. national security strategy can best be adapted if the future world proves less tractable than now hoped, and if serious competition emerges among the major powers, including with Russia and China

- how U.S. national security strategy and defense plans can best adapt if efforts to prevent further WMD proliferation and nuclear terrorism do not adequately succeed

- how a containment, deterrence, and defense strategy can best be pursued in the Middle East if Iran acquires nuclear weapons and how democratization of the region can best be pursued in an era of revolutions against tyrants

- how new-era political concepts for guiding security affairs in Europe and Asia can best be designed in ways that provide appropriate strategic guidance for handling future military commitments and related military and security issues

- how U.S. conventional forces can best be sized, configured, and modernized for the long haul in ways that are effective and affordable, and that maintain adequate capabilities for both hybrid warfare in the Middle East and high-tech deterrence and defense missions in Asia

- how future U.S. overseas forces are to be sized and designed in ways that help lead NATO in Europe, perform new-era missions in the Middle East while keeping a suitably low political profile, and achieve key security goals in Asia while adapting to China's growing anti-access and area-denial capabilities

- how new-era nuclear commitments, conventional forces, and missile defenses are to be blended together in all three regions to provide extended deterrence, reassurance of allies and partners, and crisis response capabilities

- how future U.S. nuclear forces are to be sized and structured if future negotiations produce deeper reductions than envisioned by New START

- how adequate U.S. forces and improvements are to be funded and prioritized, along with enhanced civilian capabilities and homeland security assets, in an era of tight interagency budgets and scarce resources

- how U.S. allies and partners can best be approached to elicit their support for the new regional missile defense strategy and deployments, and how shortfalls in SM–3 can best be handled

- how NATO improvements can best be pursued in an era of shrinking European defense budgets in ways that pursue reforms, efficiencies, and adequate deployable forces and capabilities

- how the forces and capabilities of allies and partners in Asia and the Middle East can best be improved and integrated in ways that produce interoperability with U.S. military forces and enhance common deterrence and defense efforts

- how the State Department's Office of Under Secretary for Political Affairs and its Bureau of Political-Military Affairs should be reformed to carry out new-era classical diplomacy.

Bottom Line. Individually and collectively, the seven official studies go a long way toward equipping the new U.S. national security strategy and defense plans with sound intellectual capital, including goals, policies, and improvement priorities. But they do not preclude the need for further thinking, analyzing, and refining. Indeed, they open the door to a new era of studies and analyses whose dimensions are now only beginning to be understood. Meeting this challenge will be a key part of handling the security, defense, diplomatic, and development agenda ahead.

National Security Strategy (Washington, DC: The White House, May 2010), available at <www.whitehouse.gov/sites/default/files/rss_viewer/national_security_strategy.pdf>.

Quadrennial Defense Review Report (Washington, DC: Department of Defense, February 2010), available at <www.defense.gov/qdr/qdr%20as%20of%2029jan10%201600.pdf>.

The QDR in Perspective: Meeting America's National Security Needs in the 21st Century, Final Report of the Quadrennial Defense Review Independent Panel, by Stephen J. Hadley and William J. Perry, co-chairmen (Washington, DC: United States Institute of Peace, 2010), available at <www.usip.org/files/qdr/qdrreport.pdf>.

Nuclear Posture Review Report (Washington, DC: Department of Defense, April 2010, available at <www.defense.gov/npr/docs/2010%20nuclear%20posture%20review%20report.pdf>.

Ballistic Missile Defense Review Report (Washington, DC: Department of Defense, February 2010), available at <www.defense.gov/bmdr/docs/BMDR%20as%20of%2026JAN10%200630_for%20web.pdf>.

NATO 2020: Assured Security; Dynamic Engagement (Brussels: NATO Public Diplomacy Division, May 2010), available at <www.nato.int/strategic-concept/expertsreport.pdf>.

Leading Through Civilian Power: The First Quadrennial Diplomacy and Development Review (Washington, DC: Department of State, December 2010), available at <www.state.gov/documents/organization/153108.pdf>.

Richard L. Kugler is a Senior Consultant to the Center for Technology and National Security Policy (CTNSP), Institute for National Strategic Studies, at the National Defense University. Formerly, Dr. Kugler was Distinguished Research Professor in CTNSP, and earlier, Director of the Department of Defense's Strategic Concepts Development Center, a Senior Executive in the Office of Secretary of Defense, and a Senior Defense Analyst at the RAND Corporation. He has been awarded the Distinguished Civilian Service Medal and other high-level decorations. He has published 17 books on national security strategy and defense planning, and multiple articles in *Foreign Affairs, Survival,* and other journals. He holds a Ph.D. from the Massachusetts Institute of Technology.

www.ingramcontent.com/pod-product-compliance
Lightning Source LLC
Chambersburg PA
CBHW070806280326
41934CB00012B/3075